MW00454410

Presented To:

_____

From:

_____

Date:

_____

GOVERNORS
OF
PRAISE

GOVERNORS
OF
PRAISE

Releasing
Heaven on Earth

JOSHUA FOWLER

DESTINY IMAGE® PUBLISHERS, INC.

P.O. Box 310, Shippensburg, PA 17257-0310

"Promoting Inspired Lives."

This book and all other Destiny Image, Revival Press, MercyPlace, Fresh Bread, Destiny Image Fiction, and Treasure House books are available at Christian bookstores and distributors worldwide.

For a U.S. bookstore nearest you, call 1-800-722-6774.

For more information on foreign distributors, call 717-532-3040.

Reach us on the Internet: www.destinyimage.com.

ISBN 13 TP: 978-0-7684-4079-9

ISBN 13 Ebook: 978-0-7684-8911-8

For Worldwide Distribution, Printed in the U.S.A.

1 2 3 4 5 6 / 14 13 12

ENDORSEMENTS

This exceptional work by Dr. Joshua Fowler is one of the most profound, yet practical approaches to this subject of praise and worship that I have read in a long time. The author's approach to this timely issue is a fresh breath of air that captivates the heart, engages the mind, and inspires the spirit. *Governors of Praise* is a gift of motivation to worship.

Dr. Myles Munroe
BFMI/MMI
Nassau, Bahamas

Dr. Fowler has written a true gem with *Governors of Praise*. I would recommend it highly to anyone who desires a greater understanding of what truly happens when we release the sound of praise. I am convinced that these concepts and teachings can truly unlock our authority in the Kingdom, as well as change the way we approach our corporate and personal times of worship. This is a must read!

Trent Cory
Minister / Worship Leader / Songwriter

In his book, *Governors of Praise,* Joshua Fowler brings to the 21st-century church a renewed understanding of the purpose and power of praise. His passion to see the Body of Christ understand and embrace their position, seated in heavenly places with Christ, will stir you to take your place as a governor of praise in the earth. Allow the truths in this book to penetrate your heart and transform your expressions of praise into prophetic decrees that shatter the enemy's territory and release the Kingdom of God!

Kelanie Gloeckler
Worship Leader / Songwriter
New Life Christian Fellowship
Jacksonville, FL

Joshua Fowler is a man of God in passionate pursuit of His Presence, and has been since he was a teenager. His breadth and depth of understanding regarding the heart of the Father, and what the Father is seeking from His sons and daughters is drawn from his wealth of study and handling of the Word of God for many, many years. He is a seasoned apostolic voice with a fresh mandate to unleash a flood tide of God's glorious river in and through the saints. *Governors of Praise* is a "hands-on" life-long learning manual for where the move of God needs to be directed and flowing in the coming days.

Dr. Mark J. Chironna

Joshua Fowler has written a book that I believe is a must read for every believer, especially pastors. I had the amazing privilege of reading *Governors of Praise* while ministering in worship gatherings across the nation of Brazil. It stirred my faith and stoked the flame in my heart to see a nation changed through the power of praise! The revelation in this book is crucial in the times that we are living. There is an urgency in this hour for us as the children of God to step into a place of governmental authority in our worship! I know Joshua Fowler personally and have ministered in his church for years. He lives what he teaches in this book. I wholeheartedly recommend *Governors of Praise;* it will challenge you and hopefully bring some new insight to the way you view the power of your praise!

Jason Lee Jones
Worship Recording Artist
www.richestoffare.com

Apostle Joshua has a calling to lead the Body of Christ into the presence of the Lord; he is gifted in this way. His new book, *Governors of Praise,* will bring you into a new dimension in praise.

I remember the first time I met him at a conference that the Lord gave me a word for him: as a drummer, he carries the heart of God, and it is released as he plays the drums. He literally releases the heartbeat of God for praise. Your life will never be the same as you engage in the revelation he shares in this book.

Apostle Mark Van Gundy
Senior Pastor
Church of Destiny and Igreja Philadelphia
London, England

Apostle Joshua Fowler is a voice to this generation. God has raised this man up as a general. *Governors of Praise* is a must read. As the Church continues to understand the power behind our praise, we will take territory for His Kingdom. In this book you will get an understanding of prophetic praise. Prophetic praise is not praising God for something that has already happened; it's praising God for something to happen. Apostle Fowler, you did it again!

J.R. Gonzalez

Apostle Joshua has truly heard from God in writing *Governors of Praise!* In an age when people are collectively spending millions on conferences and retreats to find the "outpouring" of God's presence, Apostle Joshua has brought us back to our original purpose of worshiping God and taking dominion on earth—and thus finding His "outpouring"!

Apostle Steve Perea
West Coast Five Fold Network

When I began to read this book, the image that came to mind is that I was holding a "tuning fork" in my hands. I believe that's what this book will do for your life. I believe the revelation of praise and worship is a tuning fork that brings us into unity with God and into His very manifest love and presence. I encourage you to open your heart, mind, and spirit to embrace the journey of revelation that Joshua Fowler will take you on in this book. I believe you hold in your hands some precious keys of revelation that will take you deeper in your walk with Jesus Christ!

Ryan Wyatt
Fuse Church

It is with great pleasure that I take this opportunity to endorse my friend and fellow minister Dr. Joshua Fowler's new book *Governors of Praise.*

Having known Dr. Fowler for over 12 years, I know that what is contained in the pages of this book is from a man who operates as a true "Governor of Praise." As a matter of fact, his life and ministry of praise and worship has been a tremendous blessing to us here at Dominion-Life International Ministries, the body of believers that my wife and I lead. We have written several songs, and two in particular immediately stand out in relation to Dr. Fowler:

"Governors of Praise" was written by one of our praise and worship leaders right after he ministered on that very subject at our ministry.

"Let Us Go Up" was born when he ministered at our ministry; he also assisted us in writing it!

I highly recommend *Governors of Praise* not only to church leaders but also to lay-people everywhere, who seriously desire to be grounded in understanding praise and worship! Read, then go forth, and *be* a Governor of Praise!

Michael Scantlebury, Apostle
Dominion-Life International Ministries
Founding Apostle
Kingdom-Impact International Network
Author of several books including
Leaven Revealed; I Will Build My Church—
Jesus Christ; Five Pillars of the Apostolic;
Apostolic Purity; Apostolic Reformation,
Internal Reformation; Jesus Christ the Apostle
and High Priest of Our Profession

This new book by Apostle Joshua Fowler provides a real solution for those who have been called to take territories for the Kingdom of God. It is authentic, insightful, and replete with useful strategies for releasing the power of praise in any situation. In my work as a life change strategist, I will without a doubt put this tool in the hands of those individuals, teams, and organizations who desire to realize their God-given right to take dominion. Every Kingdom practitioner should have a copy of the *Governors of Praise* in their arsenal.

Dr. Michael A. Phillips
Certified Business Advisor
Master Life Change Strategist and Senior Leader of
Kingdom Life Int'l Center, Orlando, FL

In that day I will make the governors of Judah like a firepan in the woodpile, and like a fiery torch in the sheaves; they shall devour all the surrounding peoples on the right hand and on the left, but Jerusalem shall be inhabited again in her own place—Jerusalem (Zechariah 12:6).

TABLE OF
CONTENTS

FOREWORD

I have personally seen Joshua Fowler's passion for praise, worship, and the presence of God. His passion for worship is evident in his local church, and can be seen in the people he has raised up to be true worshipers. His passion can also be seen in this book. The revelation in *Governors of Praise* is necessary for those who want to have significant breakthroughs in their personal lives, ministries, and territories.

There is an authority and power that is released through praise; this is why the book is about

Governors of Praise. Praise is a weapon, and praise is a part of ruling and reigning with Christ. Jesus comes from the tribe of Judah. The scepter comes from the tribe of Judah. God's tabernacle was in Judah. His presence was in Zion, which was located in Judah. Praisers have the spiritual DNA of Judah, the tribe from which Christ the Ruler comes.

It is more necessary than ever that leaders teach on the subject of praise. God inhabits the praises of Israel. In other words, praise brings the presence of God; the King dwells in the midst of praise. This book will challenge readers to see the importance of praise for today's church. As Joshua says, "Praise is not a preliminary part of the church service." Praise among the nations was God's ultimate plan and purpose through the redemptive act of Christ's death and sacrifice. The Lord's directive to Joshua— "Teach My people to worship Me, for worship is the closest place on earth to Me"—is the motivation for this book. God is pleased when people are taught to worship.

As you read this book, allow the inspired words to settle in your spirit. Joshua is writing from a place of prophetic authority and revelation. This is not an echo of what has been written before. There is always fresh revelation for a new generation, and Joshua is a voice to this generation. His assignment is to see a new generation arise and come forth in praise and worship that will go further than previous generations. We have yet to see the fullness of what God desires to do through *Governors of Praise*. The best is yet to come. There are miracles that are yet to be released. Get ready to go on a new journey in praise, but most of all, get ready to take your position as a Governor of Praise.

John Eckhardt, November 2011

INTRODUCTION

It was in an obscure place nestled in the middle of what appeared to be Nowhereville. As a mere 16-year-old, I had a God encounter that shook me to my core and unleashed an insatiable appetite for the presence of God. This encounter didn't happen in a large conference or in a mega-church. It didn't happen with world-renowned speakers or worship teams. It took place in a small church in the frozen farmlands of Wisconsin.

I had never witnessed anything like this before. The atmosphere was pregnant with expectancy and fueled by intense hunger and prayer. There were people coming continuously throughout the day on their breaks and walking the floors of the sanctuary, praying and singing in the Spirit. The church had a private school, and each hour the students would open the classroom doors and fall on their faces, praying and singing in the Spirit. When it came time for service, the building was so thick with the presence of God that it was as if you could have cut it with a knife! The people were not satisfied with your typical, "little dab will do you" song service but pressed in with passion until they touched the Lord.

After the Word was preached, many people came forward, giving their lives to the Lord. Instead of the pastor closing with a few remarks and prayer, he called for the worship team and commanded the people to enter in with the angels who were rejoicing over the souls that were saved. Like a volcano, the place erupted with shouting, dancing, and singing. In the midst of this, I closed my eyes, lifted my hands, let go, and began to dance. Suddenly, I was raptured into higher realms of praise and worship than I had ever experienced. Although I started out seven rows back, I was oblivious to the fact that I had praised my way all the way to the front of the building beside the keyboard. The song ended with a crescendo, and the pastor began addressing the people.

I tried to restrain myself. However, I was drunk on the new wine and couldn't stop laughing. The pastor and the church heard me and joined in on the laughter. Then my emotions overflowed, and I began to weep tears of joy. I fell to my knees, and when I touched the floor, Heaven opened, and I heard the most beautiful sounds I had ever heard! It was the Host of Heaven worshiping before God's throne. Then the Lord said something that sent me on a quest that has shaped my life's destiny. He said, "Teach My people to worship Me; for worship is the closest place on earth to Me." By this point, I was weeping and trembling uncontrollably, and all of a sudden I heard a loud boom! It was the sound of the cordless microphone jarring as Pastor John jumped off the platform and ran over to me. He placed his hand on my head and released a prophecy that still resounds in my spirit today: "I have put My Word in your mouth and a stone in your hand to set this generation free."

I believe that this book is part of the fulfillment of that prophecy and is a word and stone to set generations free. It is my desire that as you continue reading, you will be stirred to a greater hunger and passion for the Lord and that you will arise as one of God's Governors of Praise. In this book, you will learn how your praise and worship opens the heavens, draws the lost into the Kingdom, releases signs and wonders, and allows us to govern territories and impact nations for Christ! Move beyond the revelation, receive the impartation, and when the Holy Spirit moves upon your heart, enter into participation! Whether you kneel, lift your hands, sing, dance, shout, cry, or laugh, just let go and join Heaven's Host and the Governors of Praise.

1

BECOMING A GOVERNOR OF PRAISE

Did you know that praising and worshiping God is one of the most powerful things you can do? So many churches consider praise and worship to only be part of the preliminaries in a service, or at best, something that prepares people to hear the Word of God. When most Christians think of making a difference in their world, they immediately think of things like missions, outreach, or acts of service. Although these ministries are important and needed in the Body of Christ, what really will shake the nations and change lives in this day and hour is for God's people to become *Governors of Praise*.

Let's take a look at a passage of the Bible that explains this concept:

> *In that day I will make the governors of Judah like a firepan in the woodpile, and like a fiery torch in the sheaves; they shall devour all the surrounding peoples on the right hand and on the left, but Jerusalem shall be inhabited again in her own place—Jerusalem* (Zechariah 12:6).

In the very first phrase of this verse, the Lord mentions the "governors of Judah." Judah was one of the 12 tribes of Israel, but the prophecies that related to these 12 tribes are applicable to us as the Church today, the new Israel. The name *Judah* actually means "praise."[1] So this verse, Zechariah 12:6, is describing what will happen when the governors of Judah, the Governors of Praise, come forth and begin to accomplish the work that God has destined for them.

God wants you, me, and all of the members of His Church today to become Governors of Praise. He says that "in that day" (and I believe that day is now) He will make His Governors of Praise *"like a firepan in the woodpile, and like a fiery torch in the sheaves"* (Zech. 12:6). The words *fiery torch* in this verse also mean fire or lightning in the sheaves. Did you know that around the throne of God there is lightning? A lightning bolt is a powerful release of energy. Things happen around God's throne! Destinies are released; promises are fulfilled; and territories are taken for God's Kingdom. When God's Governors of Praise begin to rise up, lightning begins to strike in the heavenlies! Things begin to shift in atmospheres so people can be set free.

Verse 6 continues, *"They shall devour all the surrounding peoples on the right hand and on the left...."* The word *peoples* in this instance means "nations."[2] Do you want to see the nations come and submit themselves to the glory of God? The Word says that the knowledge of the glory of the Lord will cover the earth as the waters cover the sea (see Hab. 2:14). But that will only happen when God's Governors of Praise rise up and begin to inhabit Jerusalem through the power of the Spirit of God.

The Bible says in Ephesians 2 that we are seated together with Christ in heavenly places.

> *But God, who is rich in mercy, because of His great love with which He loved us, even when we were dead in trespasses, made us alive together with Christ (by grace you have been saved), and raised us up together, and made us sit together in the heavenly places in Christ Jesus* (Ephesians 2:4-6).

What this verse means is that we've got to take on a governmental role in our praise. Our praise is not supposed to just be words mouthed from a defeated position here on the earth. No! Our praise is supposed to take place from a position of victory, from up in the heavens, sitting in that seat that is looking down on the enemy. We don't look at the enemy here on earth in order to prophesy against something that's over us, but we take our seats as judges and as Governors in the heavens. We speak against those forces of darkness that are beneath our feet. The Bible says that God has put all things beneath the feet of Jesus (see 1 Cor. 15:25, 27; Eph. 1:22; Heb. 2:8). But the Word also says, *"The God of peace will crush Satan under your feet shortly"* (Rom. 16:20). Are you ready to see satan crushed beneath your feet? I don't know if you've got a size 11 shoe, a size 12, or even a size 4. It doesn't matter! When you become a Governor of Praise, God begins to crush satan under your feet, and you begin to walk in victory!

ENDNOTES

1. http://www.studylight.org/lex/heb/view.cgi?number=030341; Strong's # 3034; "yadah."

2. http://concordances.org/hebrew/5971a.htm; Strong's # 5971a, "`am."

2

SHUT THE DEVIL UP!

So many Christians have this common misunderstanding about praise: "Praising God builds me up and helps to strengthen my spirit." While that is certainly true, that is not all praise and worship does.

Let's take a look at one verse that will give us a greater understanding of what exactly takes place when we praise and worship God.

Out of the mouth of babes and nursing infants You have ordained strength, because of Your enemies, that You may silence the enemy and the avenger (Psalm 8:2).

When Jesus quoted this passage, He actually said, *"Out of the mouth of babes and nursing infants You have perfected praise"* (Matt. 21:16). So, *strength* and *praise* are synonymous. When you praise God, you receive strength. If you need strength, you need to praise God! The Bible says that the joy of the Lord is your strength, and you receive joy in the presence of the Lord (see Neh. 8:10). In His presence there is fullness of joy and life forevermore (see Ps. 16:11). God inhabits the praises of His people (see Ps. 22:3). So if you want more joy in your life, you have to have His presence. Once you receive His presence, you receive joy and strength for the battles you face.

In the New International Version, He says, *"From the lips of children and infants You, Lord, have called forth Your praise"* (Matt. 21:16 NIV). When we look at Psalm 8:2 in its original context, we might ask the question, "God has called forth praise for what?" The answer is clear: because of the enemies of the Lord.

This directly contradicts the idea that praise is only for us—or even for God's benefit. But God has made it clear: He has ordained praise that we might overcome the enemy, that we might still the enemy and the avenger. One way to say this is "that you might shut the devil up." Do you want to shut the devil up in your life? The answer is the praise and worship of God!

There is Governmental Praise. This is a role that you can take in the heavenlies. You can take your seat with Christ in the spiritual realm and begin to speak forth the praises of God. This implies that there is an importance attached to the words that you speak! Praising God does not include saying, "Oh Lord, please, I beg of You..." or "Oh God, I don't know if You are going to fulfill Your promises..." or "I just don't know if it's Your will...." No! Praise knows what the will of the Father is, and then it speaks forth that will into the earth. When true praise goes forth, it begins to silence the enemy!

When you are truly praising and worshiping the living God, there will be no fear in your life. You won't have any fear of the devil or what he might do to you because you will know that He who is within you is greater than he who is in the world (see 1 John 4:4). You will know beyond a shadow of a doubt that all of God's plans for you are for good, and not evil, and when you are governing your life and the territory around you in praise, His will and His good plans will come to pass!

3

TOO HOT TO HANDLE

Do you want to be too hot for the devil to handle? Do you want to be too bold for him to hold? Let's look again at our key passage to see how we can keep the enemy from gaining any kind of foothold in our lives—through praise:

> In that day I will make the **governors of Judah** like a **firepan** in the woodpile, and like a fiery torch in the sheaves; they shall devour all the surrounding peoples on the right hand and on the left,

but Jerusalem shall be inhabited again in her own place—Jerusalem (Zechariah 12:6).

The word *firepan* here can also be translated as the word *hearth*.[1] In Old Testament times, a hearth was a chafing dish for coals or a cauldron used for cooking. God says that He will make us like "hearths of fire"; in other words, He will make us into places that "cook things up" for His Kingdom. He wants us to turn up the heat in the kitchen and make it so hot that the devil can't stand to be in that kitchen anymore!

Unfortunately, today there are many churches that are lukewarm; their praise and worship is so weak that the devil has taken up residence there. Did you know that you can allow the praise and worship in your church to become so "user-friendly" that it becomes unfriendly to God? Worship is not about us; it's all about Him and what He *can* and *will* do through us when we make Him and His authority our number-one priority. We need to become God-friendly and Holy Spirit-sensitive instead of user-friendly and seeker-sensitive. Instead of being concerned with how many people we can get in the building, we need to be focused on how much of God we can attract through our worship. After all, it's when He is truly lifted up that all will be drawn to Him!

The difference can be seen when you enter a house where there are Governors of Praise operating. Devils cannot abide in that place! In that place, the people cry out, "Let God arise, and let His enemies be scattered!" (See Psalm 68:1.) When you get in a place where God is arising in the midst of the people, the enemies of God are scattered. They can't dwell in His presence. It is so wonderful to be in a church service where the presence of God is welcomed—and sickness and disease can't stay in that meeting. When someone comes in with cancer or some type of disease, it can't stay because the presence of God overwhelms the adversary.

That's what comes when you *turn up the heat!* God wants us to be on fire for Him because when we are, miracles, signs, and wonders take place. The trouble comes when we are lukewarm—neither hot nor cold. In Revelation 3, Jesus said that if we were lukewarm, then He would spew us out of His mouth (see Rev. 3:16 KJV). Many churches today are lukewarm. Jesus wants us to be hot or cold. We must decide if we're in or we're out. Are you in it to win it? Or are you just trying to survive until tomorrow, when you'll get up and do the same thing all over again?

One of the literal meanings of the word *hearth* in the Hebrew language is "a pulpit or platform."[2] God was saying that He would make the governors of

Judah, the Governors of Praise, to be like a pulpit or a platform from which He could make proclamations. God wants to make His announcements to the world from us, His Governors of Praise! When He releases those decrees and those declarations from our pulpits, it will silence the enemy in our region. See, our praise is not just for the house of God, from which it originates, but it is to go out into the atmosphere and shift the nations of the world.

In Zechariah 12:6, the word *torch* also has a special meaning. It can be translated from the Hebrew language as "to shine."[3] God wants us to arise and shine among His people today!

> *Arise, shine; for your light has come! And the glory of the Lord is risen upon you. For behold, the darkness shall cover the earth, and deep darkness the people; but the Lord will arise over you, and His glory will be seen upon you. The Gentiles shall come to your light, and kings to the brightness of your rising* (Isaiah 60:1-3).

Our light has come, and the glory of the Lord has risen upon us. The word *torch* also means a lamp or a flame.[4] It means something that is burning or is on fire. Are you ready to see something catch fire and begin to burn inside of you? Most of us, when we first got saved, felt like we were overcome with passion and zeal, but so many times, if we're not careful, our passion dies off in time.

Can you remember the zeal you used to have for God? Do you recall when you just couldn't wait to get in the presence of God? You had to be at God's house. You had to be in prayer. You had to read the Bible. Today, God is looking for people who will get back to that place where they're burning with passion for God, for His house, and for prayer.

Zechariah 12:6 tells us where the torch is to be lit: in the *sheaves*. The word *sheaf* means "a handful."[5] Do you want to see God's hands wrapped around you? When we have a handful, a grasp of God's purposes in His Body, the hand of God, the fivefold ministries, will begin to operate like never before, bringing change like lightning in the region.

A firepan in the hearth and a fiery torch in the sheaves, these are what God longs for His Governors of Praise to become in the earth! *"Your kingdom come. Your will be done on earth as it is in heaven"* (Matt. 6:10).

Just as it is in Heaven, God is raising up burning ones who will release Heaven on earth. You and I were born to burn! We are called to be people who are burning fervently with a lovesick passion for our Savior!

I watched till thrones were put in place, and the Ancient of Days was seated; His garment was white as snow, and the hair of His head was like pure wool. His throne was a fiery flame, Its wheels blazing burning fire; a fiery stream issued and came forth from before Him... (Daniel 7:9-10). (See also Hebrews 12:29; Isaiah 6:1-8; Revelation 4:1-11; 5:11; 7:1-2.)

Our God is a consuming fire, and from His fiery throne issues a river of fire. As we spend time in His presence, we will come forth in Kingdom demonstration as burning ones who are too hot to handle and too bold to hold for the forces of darkness.

ENDNOTES

1. http://www.blueletterbible.org/lang/lexicon/lexicon. cfm?strongs=H3595; Strong's # 3595, "kiyowr."

2. Ibid.

3. http://concordances.org/hebrew/3940.html; Strong's # 3940, "lappid."

4. Ibid.

5. http://concordances.org/hebrew/5995.htm; Strong's # 5995, "amir."

4

BLESSINGS
AND PROMISES

Genesis 49 lists the blessings and promises that were given to the sons of Jacob, the sons of Israel. Each son was given certain prophetic blessings, but the tribe of Judah was special. Remember, the word *Judah* means "praise." When we begin to move into the calling of praise and worship that God has for us, we will begin to see these blessings of Judah manifest in our lives and in the life of God's Church.

Judah, you are he whom your brothers shall praise; your hand shall be on the neck of your enemies; your father's children shall bow down before you. Judah is a lion's whelp; from the prey, my son, you have gone up. He bows down, he lies down as a lion; and as a lion, who shall rouse him? The scepter shall not depart from Judah, nor a lawgiver from between his feet, until Shiloh comes; and to Him shall be the obedience of the people. Binding His donkey to the vine, and His donkey's colt to the choice vine, He washed his garments in wine, and His clothes in the blood of grapes. His eyes are darker than wine, and His teeth whiter than milk (Genesis 49:8-12).

God's Word is so good! He gives us such insight and strategy on how to defeat the enemy in our lives. The first thing the Lord tells us in this passage is that the hand of Judah, or the hand of praise, will be "on" the neck of our enemies. The King James Version actually says *"thy hand shall be in the neck of thine enemies"* (Gen. 49:8). Have you ever seen a Bruce Lee movie where the hero spins around and then goes straight for the jugular of his enemy? That's what our praise can do to the devil—it can strike him right in the neck, in the jugular, in his vocal cords, even. For some of us, the lying words of the enemy need to be cast down.

When we begin to worship God with our own voices, that praise goes into the neck of our enemy and silences him. That's why God said that He's ordained praise and He's ordained strength. Why? To shut the devil up. Praise paralyzes the vocal cords of darkness and causes your enemy to scatter in the mighty name of Jesus!

There are so many benefits of becoming a Governor of Praise. Judah's father's children will bow down before him. Judah is a lion's whelp from the prey. The scepter will not depart from Judah. Where there are Governors of Praise, the scepter—the authority of the Lord—will not depart from that place. When God arises with a shout, all of His enemies are scattered, and His purposes are realized in the earth.

It is important to understand something about the scepter of Judah, the scepter of praise. When the scepter of a king or queen is extended to a person, everything that person asks for, everything he or she desires, is granted unto him or her. When the scepter was extended, Queen Esther could enter the throne room and make her petitions known. Many of us want to see God answer our prayers, but all we're doing is crying and pleading and begging Him to do something. But God says to rise up as Governors of Praise! He says, "Begin to make My name glorious, to make My praise glorious in the earth, and when you do, My scepter will stay with you, and everything you ask will be granted."

The Word says, *"The scepter shall not depart from Judah, nor a lawgiver from between his feet, until Shiloh comes; and to Him shall be the obedience of the people"* (Gen. 49:10). The King James Version says, *"And unto Him shall the gathering of the people be."* Do you want to see the gathering of nations? Do you want to see the gathering of the heathen, the gathering of the lost who are coming to God? That will take place when there are Governors of Praise seated in heavenly places with Christ, making His praise glorious.

The Church today seems to value marketing programs. We have become "user-friendly," often more focused on building a social club than the Kingdom of God. It is possible to have a "golden calf society" in a church where everybody shines one another's armor and looks pretty. In that case, we can all become navel-gazers and never actually accomplish anything for the Kingdom. But when people rise up and begin to praise God, religious folk begin to leave, devils begin to scream, and God's Kingdom is established, His scepter is extended, and the lost truly begin to be gathered in!

Jesus said, *"And I, if I am lifted up from the earth, will draw all peoples to Myself"* (John 12:32). When we praise and worship Jesus Christ, the lost from all nations of the earth will be drawn to the Father. Jesus says to

His Church: "When I find some Governors of Praise, when I find some people who will sit with Me in heavenly places, when I find some people who will make My praise glorious, there will My scepter be. There will I rise and draw all people unto Myself."

When my son, Hunter, was 12 years old, he did a project on magnets in his Christian school. His teachers asked him to compare magnets with God. That was an easy project! I found many Scriptures to help him—so many that he began to say, "Thanks, Dad—that's enough!" The truth is, the Bible is filled with references to the "magnetism" of God. God has said that when we draw nigh to Him, He will draw nigh to us (see James 4:8; Matt. 18:20). When we begin to praise the Lord, when we begin to love on Jesus, and when we begin to glorify the Father, He will glorify us (see Jer. 30:19). He will glorify His house, the Church, with His glory (see John 17:20-23). When there is a people who will draw close to Him and will lift Him up, He says He will draw people to Himself (see John 12:32). If you have a desire, a longing, to see lost people come to Jesus, then begin to praise Him in your life, and watch how He begins to move to save people and deliver them!

5

"JAILHOUSE ROCK"

The true Gospel is not a "user-friendly" Gospel. Many people believe that when they come to Christ, all of their problems will be solved. Nothing could be further from the truth! The Bible tells of many believers who were persecuted for their faith.

Who through faith subdued kingdoms, wrought righteousness, obtained promises, stopped the mouths of lions, quenched the violence of fire, escaped the edge of the sword, out of weakness were made strong, waxed valiant in fight, turned to flight the armies of the aliens. Women received their dead raised to life again: and others were tortured, not accepting deliverance; that they might obtain a better resurrection: and others had trial of cruel mockings and scourgings, yea, moreover of bonds and imprisonment: They were stoned, they were sawn asunder, were tempted, were slain with the sword: they wandered about in sheepskins and goatskins; being destitute, afflicted, tormented; (of whom the world was not worthy:) they wandered in deserts, and in mountains, and in dens and caves of the earth. And these all, having obtained a good report through faith, received not the promise: God having provided some better thing for us, that they without us should not be made perfect (Hebrews 11:33-40 KJV).

For I think that God has displayed us, the apostles, last, as men condemned to death; for we have been made a spectacle to the world, both to angels and to men. We are fools for Christ's sake, but you are wise in Christ! We are weak, but you are strong! You are distinguished, but we are dishonored! To the present hour we both hunger and thirst, and we are poorly clothed, and beaten, and homeless. Being reviled, we bless; being persecuted, we endure; being defamed, we entreat. We have been made as the filth of the world, the offscouring of all things until now (1 Corinthians 4:9-13).

I know how to be abased, and I know how to abound. Everywhere and in all things I have learned both to be full and to be hungry, both to abound and to suffer need (Philippians 4:12).

Are they ministers of Christ?——I speak as a fool——I am more: in labors more abundant, in stripes above measure, in prisons more frequently, in deaths often. From the Jews five times I received forty stripes minus one. Three times I was beaten with rods; once I was stoned; three times I was shipwrecked; a night and a day I have been in the deep; in journeys often, in perils of waters, in perils of robbers, in perils of my own countrymen, in perils of the Gentiles, in perils in the city, in perils in the wilderness, in perils in the sea, in perils among false brethren; in weariness and toil, in sleeplessness often, in hunger and thirst, in fastings often, in cold and nakedness—— besides the other things, what comes upon me daily: my deep concern for all the churches (2 Corinthians 11:23-28).

But we have this treasure in earthen vessels, that the excellence of the power may be of God and not of us. We are hard-pressed on every side, yet not crushed; we are perplexed, but not in despair; persecuted, but not forsaken; struck down, but not destroyed——always carrying about in the body the dying of the Lord Jesus, that the life of Jesus also may be manifested in our body (2 Corinthians 4:7-10).

I like to say that when you accept Christ, you're going to catch hell—but you don't have to hold on to it!

Now I appreciate everything that the Word of Faith movement has done for the Church. Certainly there is a lot of truth in the fact that the words you speak in your situation will help to shape that situation in your life. But when people come up with the misguided notion that everything will be perfect if they just have enough faith to overcome, unfortunately, they have taken the teaching to the extreme. That doctrine is not taught in the Scripture. So many of us want to know God in the power of His resurrection, but we forget that we must also participate in the fellowship of His sufferings. We believe that if we just have enough faith, we won't have to go through certain situations. I think the apostle Paul would have had to disagree!

Throughout the course of his ministry, Paul wrote two-thirds of the New Testament, established churches throughout the known world, and preached to and saw hundreds of people converted. But he also faced imprisonment, stoning, shipwreck, and snake bites! We all say we want to be like the apostle Paul—until it's time for the persecution. Paul was a man of faith and a man of power, but he ended up in jail.

Let's take a look at what happened:

Now it happened, as we went to prayer, that a certain slave girl possessed with a spirit of divination met us, who brought her masters much profit by fortune-telling. This girl followed Paul and us, and cried out, saying, "These men are the servants of the Most High God, who proclaim to us the way of salvation." And this she did for many days. But Paul, greatly annoyed, turned and said to the spirit, "I command you in the name of Jesus Christ to come out of her." And he came out that very hour. But when her masters saw that their hope of profit was gone, they seized Paul and Silas and dragged them into the marketplace to the authorities (Acts 16:16-19).

In most cases, we would believe that casting a demon out of a person and setting her free would be a *good* thing. But at this time, Paul was being persecuted for ministering the love and the power of Jesus Christ.

And they brought them to the magistrates, and said, "These men, being Jews, exceedingly trouble our city; and they teach customs which are not lawful for us, being Romans, to receive or observe." Then the multitude rose up together against them; and the magistrates tore off their clothes and commanded them to be beaten with rods. And when they had laid many stripes on them, they threw them into prison, commanding the jailer to keep them securely. Having received such a charge, he put them into the inner prison and fastened their feet in the stocks (Acts 16:20-24).

What would most of us do in a situation like this? What would you do? I think most of us would whine and complain—but not Paul and Silas.

But at midnight Paul and Silas were praying and singing hymns to God, and the prisoners were listening to them. Suddenly there was a great earthquake, so that the foundations of the prison were shaken; and immediately all the doors were opened and everyone's chains were loosed. And the keeper of the prison, awaking from sleep and seeing the prison doors open, supposing the prisoners had fled, drew his sword and was about to kill himself. But Paul called with a loud voice, saying, "Do yourself no harm, for we are all here." Then he called for a light, ran in, and fell down trembling before Paul and Silas. And he brought them out and said, "Sirs, what must I do to be saved?" So they said, "Believe on the Lord Jesus Christ, and you will be saved, you and your household." Then they spoke the word of the Lord to him and to all who were in his house. And he took them the same hour of the night and washed their stripes. And immediately he and all his family were baptized. Now when he had brought them into his house, he set food before them; and he rejoiced, having believed in God with all his household (Acts 16:25-34).

Historians tell us that the sewers of the day ran directly through the Roman jails. Paul and Silas were very likely being held in the lower parts of the dungeon, where the stench of the sewer was running by their feet…perhaps even *over* their feet. They were in shackles. They were in bondage. Historians have also said that many times the Roman jailers would leave prisoners in stocks and bonds long after they were dead, so perhaps Paul and Silas were strapped in chains directly next to corpses in the stocks on either side of them. Can you imagine? Most people in the Church today would have given up at that point. In fact, many of us will give up if we get an unexpected bill in the mail, and if somebody talks badly about us, we call that persecution. Persecution in the Bible was when Christians were boiled in hot water and tar! When the flesh of believers was pulled from their bones—that was persecution.

But the apostle Paul and Silas, even in the midst of their terrible situation, said, "Let's sing and praise God!" The Bible says that when they prayed and sang praises to God, the place was shaken. Glory to God! Do you want to see things begin to shake around you? Begin to praise the Lord in your situation and watch things begin to move!

You might be familiar with the song made famous by Elvis Presley, "Jailhouse Rock." Well, I am telling you, he wasn't the original writer of that song! Paul and Silas wrote the original "Jailhouse Rock." That song was written when Paul and Silas began to praise God in the midnight hour. The place began to shake, and there was a jailhouse rock. The doors swung open, and the Bible says that not only were Paul and Silas set free, but *everyone* in the prison was also set free. And even the jailer, the one who had been persecuting them, was led, along with his family, to the Lord.

Remember what the Lord said in Genesis 49:10, I'm going to make you a hearth of fire. I'm going to cause all nations to come to you! There will be a gathering of the people where there's praise.

When you begin to praise God, prison doors open. If you go to your job and you whine and cry about how lost everyone is, nothing is going to happen. But if you go to your job and get there a few minutes early and praise God over that place, anoint that place with prayer, and take your lunch break and go out and pray in the break room, I guarantee that you'll start shifting the heavens over that place because you're taking your seat—a rightful seat in the heavenly places.

Look at Amos 9:11:

> *On that day I will raise up the tabernacle of David, which has fallen down, and repair its damages; I will raise up its ruins, and rebuild it as in the days of old.*

What was it like in the days of old? Stop and think about it for a moment. In the days of old, 24/7, 365 days a year, there was continuous praise. There were some 3,000 musicians who were appointed and paid to stay at the house of God and constantly praise God. But David went beyond his dispensation—he went into another dispensation and recognized that he would offer up a more excellent sacrifice than that of goats and lambs. He would offer up the sacrifice of praise. And from this praise, all the battles that Joshua didn't win, David went on to be victorious in, conquering all of the enemies. Why? Because he brought in the tabernacle of David and established it; he brought in the Ark of the Covenant and said, "We're going to minister to God continuously in this place!" From that point on, every enemy and adversary of God was put under their feet.

Do you want to see every enemy that's coming against you put beneath your feet? Follow what David did. David established the place of praise, to worship God continually. But now take a look at verse 12:

"That they may possess the remnant of Edom, and all the Gentiles who are called by My name," says the Lord who does this thing.

Notice those words: "that they may possess." Are you a possessor? Do you have in your possession the promises of the Lord? Verse 13 continues:

"Behold, the days are coming," says the Lord, "When the plowman shall overtake the reaper, and the treader of grapes him who sows seed; the mountains shall drip with sweet wine, and all the hills shall flow with it."

When David's fallen tent is restored, when the praises of God are raised again, the people will rise up as Governors of Praise and establish God's throne. The scepter of the Lord will be extended over regions and over territories so that the heathen will come to know the God of the universe. Do you want to see the new wine of God in the house? Do you want to see the praise of the Lord make a difference in the lives of your loved ones, your family members, your nation, and the world? Do you want to receive the land and the promises that God has for you? Praise is what will put you into that land and keep you there!

This isn't just an Old Testament promise. Take a look at what James told the brethren in Acts 15:16-18:

> *"'After this I will return and will rebuild the tabernacle of David, which has fallen down; I will rebuild its ruins, and I will set it up; so that the rest of mankind may seek the Lord, even all the Gentiles who are called by My name, says the Lord who does all these things.' Known to God from eternity are all His works."*

The tabernacle of David has fallen down, but God promises to restore it and set it up. God is saying in this hour, "I need some Governors of Praise...I need some people who will arise and will build Me a tabernacle of worship." Why? So people will seek after the Lord! From the beginning of the world, my friend, God planned there to be a Davidic company that would arise in this hour—governors of Judah, Governors of Praise, who would raise up the tabernacle of David so the lost would be able to come to the saving knowledge of Jesus. These "pre-believers" are going to come to know our God! Do you have any unsaved loved ones? God's promise is for you: there are pre-believers in your life who are going to come to know God because you are arising as a Governor of Praise!

6

THREE PHASES
OF PRAISE

The Lord has given this word to me: there are three phases of praise through which His people must pass. These words are not together just because they rhyme and work well together. I was praying in my prayer language one day, and these words came up out of my spirit. I know they are from the living God, and they are a powerful word to help God's people become the Governors of Praise He has called them to be.

PHASE NUMBER ONE: PENETRATION

When you begin to move into praise, you have to penetrate through the forces of darkness with your praise into the heavenlies and take your rightful place in the Kingdom of God.

PHASE NUMBER TWO: SATURATION

In the saturation phase, once you have penetrated into the Holy of Holies, you are saturated with His presence.

PHASE NUMBER THREE: PERMEATION

In the third phase of praise, you become so saturated, so filled with the Spirit, that you permeate with God's presence in the earth.

God wants you to rise up to His throne in praise; that's the only way you will be able to accomplish what He wants to do through you. You must enter into His gates with thanksgiving and His courts with praise. The only way you can enter God's presence is if you go in praise. When you enter His courts with praise, He begins to saturate you with His glory. And then He sends you back down to the earth to rain on the dry land and permeate the world with His presence.

So many people in the Church today have been praying for rain. "O God," we pray, "send Your rain!" But when you prayed that prayer, you didn't know you were actually praying for yourself! *You* are the rain. You are the rain that God wants to shower on a dry and thirsty land!

God's Word is so powerful, and it tells us what the rain—you and I—can accomplish for God's Kingdom:

> *"For My thoughts are not your thoughts, nor are your ways My ways," says the Lord. "For as the heavens are higher than the earth, so are My ways higher than your ways, and My thoughts than your thoughts. For as the rain comes down, and the snow from heaven, and do not return there, but water the earth, and make it bring forth and bud, that it may give seed to the sower and bread to the eater, so shall My word be that goes forth from My mouth; it shall not return to Me void, but it shall accomplish what I please, and it shall prosper in the thing for which I sent it"* (Isaiah 55:8-11).

God's ways are higher than our ways, and His thoughts are greater than our thoughts! But as the rain that comes down, so is God's Word, His *Rhema*. It goes out and accomplishes His purposes in the earth. It gives seed to the sower and bread to the eater. Through these verses, God is showing us how true praise is formed. It is formed in the earth and released in the earth when we come into the place of praise.

Have you ever wondered how rain actually takes place? There is barometric pressure in the earth that causes a gravitational pull, and the heavens begin to lick up from the earth what is in the earth—what is in the ocean, the lakes, and the rivers. This pressure draws the water up into the heavens, and when the pressure gets to the right point, what it has pulled up from the earth, it releases back onto the earth. So for rain to exist, there has to first be water already present on the earth that can be pulled up and released back down.

Can you see the parallel in the spiritual realm? God is saying to us today, "I am looking in the earth for people who have My Word in their mouths, who know how to speak forth praise so I can pull it up into Heaven, rain it back down, and release change in the earth!"

In Matthew 4, Jesus spoke forth the Word of God when He was facing temptation from the enemy, and in the process, He gave us an example of the power of proceeding praise:

> Then Jesus was led up by the Spirit into the wilderness to be tempted by the devil. And when He had fasted forty days and forty nights, afterward He was hungry. Now when the tempter came to Him, he said, "If You are the Son of God, command that these stones become bread." But He answered and said, "It is written: 'Man

shall not live by bread alone, but by every word that proceeds from the mouth of God'"(Matthew 4:1-4).

When Jesus successfully dealt with the enemy, He said the words, *"It is written..."* Then He quoted the Scripture: *"Man shall not live by bread alone, but by every word that proceeds from the mouth of God."* This is the proceeding Word of God, the proceeding praise that will move mountains, defeat the enemy, and usher in the Kingdom of God on the earth.

When true Governors of Praise begin to rise up and take their place in the Church, God's scepter is extended, and His Kingdom is established. God begins to feed off of the proceeding Word that is coming forth from their bellies. As the Word says, *"Out of his belly shall flow rivers of living water"* (John 7:38 KJV). God begins to pull from the rivers of living water that are in us and release them to His throne. The Book of Revelation states that there is a river that flows from God's throne, but it comes from us to Him and then back to us, just like the natural rain that we experience upon the earth.

What goes up must come down. If nothing's going up, nothing's coming down. If your mouth is shut, or if all you're sending out into the spiritual environment is murmuring and complaining, then that's all you will get back from the heavens. But when you send praise up to God's throne, up into the heavens, then that praise is going to come back down and bless your life. It will go up into the spiritual atmosphere like condensation, but when it comes back down, it will drench you in an outpouring of blessing! When you send forth proceeding praise, it's the proceeding Word of God—and it will not return void. Man shall not live by bread alone but by every word that proceeds out of the mouth of God.

You'll never proceed into your destiny until there's a proceeding Word that advances before you. But when there's a proceeding Word, the entrance of His Word into your life, it will go forth and give you entrance into your destiny, the wonderful, amazing things that God has for you.

Many people today are looking for their destiny. They're looking for breakthrough, but they're not willing to take their seat in heavenly places as Governors of Praise. Once we pay the price and become Governors of Praise, we will begin to penetrate into the heavenlies. God will saturate us with His glory, and we'll begin to permeate His presence. Then, once we have reached the phase of permeation, the place that once was dry will begin to receive the rain from our lives. The *r-a-i-n* will cause us to *r-e-i-g-n* in the earth. We become His rain, and we will become His reign. We will begin to reign and to rule in the earth!

7

GOVERNOR NEHEMIAH

But one of the elders said to me, "Do not weep. Behold, the Lion of the tribe of Judah, the Root of David, has prevailed to open the scroll and to loose its seven seals" (Revelation 5:5).

When you rise up as a Governor of Praise, it has ramifications not just for you but also for future generations. Do you want to see your children blessed? Become a Governor of Praise. Do you want to see your grandchildren blessed? Become a Governor of Praise. Don't just sit back and not participate when you come to church. When you come into the house of God—even in your own home, your living room, or your car—be militant with praise! Lift your hands, clap your hands, and shout unto God with a voice of triumph. It's not about your own nature anymore. It's about the nature of the King of the Lion of the tribe of Judah who lives inside of you.

You're a dead man or woman walking now. You don't have authority over your life anymore. You've been bought with a price. You've been bought with the shed blood of Jesus Christ. But now that you've been bought with His blood, act like He has control over your life. Allow the Word of God to "brainwash" you—to renew your mind and change your thinking. The Word is better than a bar of Dial soap for washing your mind. When you begin to speak it forth out of your mouth, it will wash your thoughts and attitudes, until after a while you'll start acting like Christ and stop acting like yourself. When you get enough of the Word in you, you'll start changing. When you come to church, your attitude won't be, *I have to praise God today; it will be, I have the high privilege and honor to praise God today!* When you get up in the morning, you'll recognize that you don't *have* to seek God early in the morning—you *get* to seek God before the cares and problems of the day begin.

When you become a Governor of Praise, there will be an intensity, a passion, and a fervency that will come forth in your relationship with the Father. The Word says that the effectual, fervent prayer of a righteous man avails much. The word *fervent* in that verse means "to be boiling hot," "to the boiling point," or "to boil over."[1] People who are Governors of Praise have reached a boiling point in their lives. They're always hot—on fire for the things of God! Are you too hot to handle and too bold for the devil to hold? Too many Christians spend their lives being lukewarm. But Jesus said, "If you're lukewarm, I will vomit you right out of My mouth!" (see Rev. 3:16). He'd rather that you are either hot or cold—but to be a Governor of Praise on the earth today, we must be on fire for Him!

This isn't about you. This is about a harvest. Governors of Praise draw the lost people of the world to the Lord. Those who don't know Jesus will be drawn to the brightness of our rising and the praise of God on our lips and in our lives. It is your destiny and your legacy to be a Governor of Praise. God preordained your life and set it up so you would be right where you are at this specific time in history.

There are several Governors of Praise depicted in the Scriptures, each of whom can become a pattern for your own life and destiny. However, we will focus on Governor Nehemiah in this chapter.

> *These lived in the days of Joiakim the son of Jeshua, the son of Jozadak, and in the days of Nehemiah the governor, and of Ezra the priest, the scribe* (Nehemiah 12:26).

Nehemiah was a governor, a person who was appointed to rule over regions and territories, just as we are called to do in our own generation. Jesus is called the King of kings. Which "kings" is He the "King" of? The Word does not refer to a figurative king out in the world who is ruling politically over nations; no, it is referring to believers. We are kings and priests unto our God. He is the King of kings. He's the Governor of governors. And His people are His Governors of Praise.

Nehemiah 2 paints a picture that will help us to understand the life of Nehemiah as a governor.

> *Then I said to them, "You see the distress that we are in, how Jerusalem lies waste, and its gates are burned with fire. Come and let us build the wall of Jerusalem, that we may no longer be a reproach." And I told them of the hand of my God which had been good upon me,*

and also of the king's words that he had spoken to me... (Nehemiah 2:17-18).

In our day, we could replace the word *Jerusalem* with whatever town or city in which we live. Without the gates of praise built up in our cities and nation, we can become a reproach. Governors are builders. They themselves are builders, and they inspire others to build as well.

So they said, "Let us rise up and build." Then they set their hands to this good work (Nehemiah 2:18).

Children of God, *Governors of Praise,* you have to strengthen your hands for this good work. What is the work that God has called *you* to do? What is your destiny in Him? Strengthen your hands and prepare for it. Whatever He calls you to do will be a good work— and you will be able to accomplish it when you release His power and blessing into your life through praise.

But when Sanballat the Horonite, Tobiah the Ammonite official, and Geshem the Arab heard of it, they laughed at us and despised us, and said, "What is this thing that you are doing? Will you rebel against the king?" So I answered them, and said to them, "The God of heaven Himself will prosper us; therefore we His servants will arise and build..." (Nehemiah 2:19-20).

It's inevitable that, just as Nehemiah did, you will face opposition, but be encouraged. God will prosper you, and you will "arise and build"!

E N D N O T E

1. 1828 Noah Webster Dictionary, "fervent," http://www.1828-dictionary.com/d/search/word,fervent.

8

THE SEAT OF
LEGAL AUTHORITY

Did you know that Governors of Praise proceed over legal matters in the heavenly realms? When you become a Governor of Praise and take your seat of legal authority, you can bring the destiny of God to pass in your life.

Take a look at what the apostle Paul said in Ephesians 2:

> *But God, who is rich in mercy, because of His great love with which He loved us, even when we were dead*

in trespasses, made us alive together with Christ (by grace you have been saved), and raised us up together, and made us sit together in the heavenly places in Christ Jesus (Ephesians 2:4-6).

You have a "heavenly seat." You have been granted a heavenly seat of authority. As a governor of Judah, as a Governor of Praise, you have been granted a seat with Him in heavenly places. God wants you to proceed... He wants you to rule from this seat.

Praise causes you to possess the land. It's important for you to understand that if you're not praising, you're not possessing. You cease to possess when you cease to praise. The Book of Judges helps us to understand this principle:

And the Lord said, "Judah shall go up. Indeed I have delivered the land into his hand" (Judges 1:2).

Praise will cause you to ascend. Praise will cause you to go up into greater things in the Lord! God says that He has delivered the land into the hand of praise. The land is delivered to a people of praise. Do you want to see your city and your nation come into the hands of the people of God? Praise will possess the land.

So Judah said to Simeon his brother, "Come up with me to my allotted territory, that we may fight against the Canaanites; and I will likewise go with you to your allotted territory." And Simeon went with him (Judges 1:3).

The name *Simeon* means "hearer."[1] Praise says to the hearers, "Come with me!" The Bible says, *"Simeon went with him."* The hearers go with the praisers. The Bible tells us that faith comes by hearing and hearing by the Word of the Lord (see Rom. 10:17). So when we begin to lift up God's praise, it releases a sound so people will have an ear to hear what the Spirit is saying. The Church will begin to hear that sound, and God's people will go up together to take the land.

Then Judah went up, and the Lord delivered the Canaanites and the Perizzites into their hand... (Judges 1:4).

There is a breakthrough anointing that is released into the lives of people who are Governors of Praise. But in order to really govern over the heavenlies, you've got to go up! You've got to rise up in the Spirit and take your rightful place in the Kingdom. You can't praise from down in the earthly realm, in the middle of your problems and your circumstances. You've got to praise from on high—from the realm of the Spirit where the blessings and the anointing of God are released. That's the true place where you will be able to govern in the spirit realm. We are seated with Christ in heavenly places.

Have you ever noticed that when you go into a courtroom, the judge is almost always seated up much higher than the rest of the people? When the judge enters the room and moves to his seat, everyone rises for the honorable judge. When the judge sits, then everyone else can sit. Our Judge, our Advocate with the Father, is Christ Jesus. Jesus is at the right hand of the Father, ever interceding for you and me, and He takes His seat there in the heavenly realm. Now, not until Christ's work on the cross, when the veil in the Temple was rent in two, has there ever been a priest who was able to take his seat. But because the work is finished, because Jesus said, "It is finished" on the cross, He is now seated at the right hand of the Father. And because He's seated in heavenly places, we, too, can take our seat in the heavenly places with Him.

The purpose for us being seated in heavenly places is so that we can *proceed*. We are there to proceed over matters.

Proceed is defined by the dictionary as a word meaning "to go forward."[2] Do you want to go forward in your life? Are you tired of spinning your tires? It is important to realize that motion is not necessarily progress! You can be in motion and still be moving around in circles or just spinning your tires. But God wants you to have forward momentum in your life!

The dictionary goes on to say: "especially after an interruption." Do you feel like you've been interrupted lately? Be honest! Sometimes it can feel like you're going somewhere, but you get interrupted on the way. God is about to give you momentum to make up for that time that's been lost. You're about to proceed forward! You may not have been getting to where God wants you to go. It may seem like you've lost sight of your purpose in life, but God's about to give you traction. Where it seems you've been stuck and your tires have been spinning, you're about to move forward!

Second, *proceed* means "to begin to carry on an action or a process." Third, it means "to move on in an orderly manner." God wants you to proceed forward in an orderly manner. Fourth, it means "to come from a source; to originate." Now what does it mean when we begin to look at the word *proceed* in the verse that says "man shall not live by bread alone, but by every word that *proceedeth*—that begins, that originates— out of the mouth of God"? We can begin to recognize that the word that originated with God is what we must live by! That word comes to us from the throne, and we live by that word. It is our sustenance. That word is how we live.

The fifth definition of *proceed* is especially important; it refers to the law and means "to institute and conduct legal action." Are you ready to rise up and take legal action against your adversary? This does not mean just praying, "Oh God, please let this happen, if it be Your will." You're not *petitioning*. You are *decreeing*. You are *declaring*. You're passing sentence on your enemy.

Let's take a look at what this means in a familiar verse to many Christians today, Isaiah 54:17:

"No weapon formed against you shall prosper, and every tongue which rises against you in judgment you shall condemn. This is the heritage of the servants of the Lord, and their righteousness is from Me," says the Lord.

This verse literally means that you will pass sentence on, make a declaration or a decree against, and silence your enemies! Even if the weapon is fully formed—even if the enemy gets it all the way built—it will not prosper against you. And every tongue that rises against you in judgment, you will condemn.

Let's look at Second Corinthians 10:3-5:

For though we walk in the flesh, we do not war according to the flesh. For the weapons of our warfare are not carnal but mighty in God for pulling down strongholds, casting down arguments and every high thing that exalts itself against the knowledge of God, bringing every thought into captivity to the obedience of Christ.

This is the Word of the Lord! God has given you a seat in the heavenlies, and it's your job to pass sentence over the words that the enemy has released concerning your life. The enemy has said to you, "You'll never be anything. You'll never amount to anything. You'll never own anything. You'll never go to any nations. You're not going to fulfill your destiny!" But because these are the words of the enemy, you can know that the exact opposite of what he's said is the truth!

If he told you that you *weren't* going to go to the nations, it should let you know to get your passport ready! If he told you that you would never own a house, you should begin to rejoice because now you know that you're going to own many houses. He told you that you wouldn't have a car, but get ready—you're about to have three or four cars, because the exact opposite of what he said is true!

But you can't just let those words against your destiny stay up there in the air. When you begin to see those thoughts and imaginations rise up, you have the authority as a Governor of Praise to stand up and silence the enemy. We learned from Psalm 8 that praise releases strength. Out of the mouth of babes He's ordained strength, or praise, so you can silence the mouth of the avenger—so that you might shut the devil up!

The call of the prophet in Jeremiah 1 gives us even further insight:

> *Then the Lord put forth His hand and touched my mouth, and the Lord said to me: "Behold, I have put My words in your mouth. See, I have this day set you over the nations and over the kingdoms, to root out and to pull down, to destroy and to throw down, to build and to plant"* (Jeremiah 1:9-10).

The word *set* in verse 10 means "to set over." It also means "to be made an overseer," "to be appointed." The Hebrew word for *set* is *paqad* and is also translated as governor.[3] God has set you over the nations and over kingdoms as a Governor of Praise! Now, this does not just refer the political kingdoms of this world. It is also referring to the kingdoms of darkness. It can also mean the kingdoms of the marketplace, or other "kingdoms" in our society today: athletics, Hollywood, the news media. God is giving you the authority to reside and to proceed over matters concerning kingdoms—to root out and to pull down, to destroy and to throw down, and to build and to plant. And the good news is that He tells you *how!*

As we have seen, "to proceed" means to institute and conduct legal action. Proceedings include a course of action or a procedure; a sequence of events occurring at a particular place or occasion. It can include legal action or litigation and the instituting or conducting of legal action. God releases His legal action, His authority, to people who are rising up in praise.

Governmental anointing is given to those who praise the Lord. Governors of Praise are able to rise up and proceed over legal matters. Are you ready to silence the forces of darkness in your region and your life? You can do so when you are a Governor of Praise. Governors of Praise rise up in the ranks. Governors of Praise have favor with God and with man. Governors of Praise don't just sit around waiting for things to happen—they make things happen! Governors of Praise are leaders. If you want to be a leader, become a Governor of Praise. If you can't praise God, you don't have any business leading in the Church. If you can't praise God, it doesn't matter how talented you are— you don't have anything to say.

On the other hand, when you rise up in praise, you are lining up with the Lion of Judah. You receive the law-giving anointing, the scepter of authority, and you move into heavenly places where you can proceed over legal affairs.

E N D N O T E S

1. http://concordances.org/hebrew/8095.htm; "Shimon"; from the root word, "Shama": http://concordances.org/hebrew/8085.htm.

2 All definitions for "proceed" taken from 1828 Noah Webster Dictionary, http://www.1828-dictionary.com/d/search/word,proceed; and the Merriam-Webster Dictionary, http://www.merriam-webster.com/dictionary/proceed.

3. http://concordances.org/hebrew/6485.htm; "paqad."

9

PROCEED THROUGH PRAISE

According to John 15, there is a proceeding Word that comes from the Father—and that is the Holy Spirit.

But when the Helper comes, whom I shall send to you from the Father, the Spirit of truth who proceeds from the Father, He will testify of Me. And you will also bear witness, because you have been with Me from the beginning (John 15:26-27).

The Spirit of truth proceeds from the Father; the Holy Spirit is a *proceeding Spirit*. He *proceeds* from the Father. He testifies of Jesus, and we do as well because we have been with Jesus Himself! Although Jesus is speaking here about His earthly disciples, in the spiritual realm, He is also referring to us, His future disciples.

Jesus said He would send the Comforter Himself. Did you ever stop to realize that the Holy Spirit is a "sent Spirit"? And when you receive this "proceeding Spirit," you receive a proceeding word. You receive the right to proceed forward and advance so you can begin to proceed over the matters in your life.

Jesus also said that the Holy Spirit would testify of Him and that we also would bear witness because we have been with Him from the beginning. How long have you "been with" Jesus? You've been with Him from the beginning. You didn't just arrive. You were sent here. You were breathed from the Father into the earth. Before you came to the earth, you were with Him. That's why every day you're growing closer to God and moving back into the idea of how things truly were before you came here. Some people call it déjà vu, but it's not—it's actually something that I call a "sonship moment."

Before we were born, we were with the Father as sons of God. We were with Him in Heaven, and when He sent us to earth, He sent us for such a time as this. There's a legacy that He's been building, and before you were ever born, the Father was breathing things into you. When you were in the lap of the Father, with your head on His chest in the Spirit, He began to release His heartbeat into your life. Then when you came forth from the birth canal of your mother's womb, when you gave your first cry, He knew what you would become (see Jer. 1). The Father was intimately involved with you, sowing things into your life. Seeds and spiritual DNA were planted inside of you, like a time capsule, and they are waiting to open up in a certain time. Now God is beginning to allow those things to erupt in your spirit, and you are beginning to have an understanding of them—even though they were already there before you came into the earth.

God sent you here to the earth in just this very time to proceed over matters. You didn't just show up! You have legal access. You have legal rights. You were sent by the Father. There's never been a greater time in history. I know that as they look down from Heaven, the apostles Paul, Peter, and John wish they could trade places with us!

We are the generation that has the Internet, Facebook, and Twitter, and we can literally touch the world with one push of a button. We can talk to the world with one camera that goes around the world through television satellites. We have cell phones, and we can talk to virtually anyone in the world at any time. Generations back, it took years to get the word out to different places. We're a chosen generation—chosen to proceed over legal matters in the Spirit.

10

DESTINED
TO REIGN

Man shall not live by bread alone, but by
every word that proceeds from the mouth of
God (Matthew 4:4).

Did you know that you, I, and every other person
in the world are proceeding words from the Father?
You're here because you were spoken into existence.
The Bible says that when God spoke, the things He
created were good, and when He created man, it was
"very good" (see Gen. 1–2). When you were spoken into

existence, that same creative power was placed inside of you, so you can lock into Heaven's frequency and receive the proceeding praise of the Father. You have the ability to receive the proceeding words of Heaven!

God spoke you into being. You were not just born—you have a purpose! You proceeded out of the very mouth of God and have been sent into the earth for such a time as this. But God has also placed a demand on you—a divine assignment that only you can fulfill. He draws you to Himself. The Bible says that no man can come unless he is "drawn" by the Spirit: *"No one can come to Me unless the Father who sent Me draws him"* (John 6:44).

God draws you, and then you follow after Him and His plans and purposes for your life. The Holy Spirit begins to woo you, and as you draw nigh to Him, He draws nigh to you.

God places the proceeding praise in our mouths, and it will cause the release of not His r-a-i-n, but His r-e-i-g-n in the earth.

Deuteronomy tells us:

And you shall remember that the Lord your God led you all the way these forty years in the wilderness, to humble you and test you, to know what was in your heart, whether you would keep His commandments or not. So He humbled you, allowed you to hunger, and fed you with manna which you did not know nor did your fathers know, that He might make you know that man shall not live by bread alone; but man lives by every word that proceeds from the mouth of the Lord (Deuteronomy 8:2-3).

This is actually the passage of Scripture that Jesus quoted when He was in the wilderness experiencing temptation by satan. Man does not live by bread (earthly food) alone; we need the proceeding word from God. We need to take that proceeding word from the heavenlies, transform it into praise, and watch change take place in our lives. The currency of Heaven is praise. When you praise God, it causes the Kingdom reign to fall upon the earth. As soon as God's Word that is proceeding to you is transformed into praise through God's living vessels on earth, then it has the right and the dominion to bring about change. Your circumstances must bow when proceeding praise is released through your lips!

The Message Bible puts it like this: *"It takes more than bread to stay alive. It takes a steady stream of words from God's mouth"* (Matt. 4:4). We all need a steady stream of words from God's mouth! We need more than just a little dab here and there—we need a steady, ongoing, daily stream of words from God, which we then transform into proceeding praise and change our lives and our world for His glory!

Proceeding praise is based on the overflow. As Revelation 22:1 states, *"And he showed me a pure river of water of life, clear as crystal, proceeding from the throne of God and of the Lamb."* God's proceeding word is like a river. The Bible says many times that when God speaks, His voice is like the sound of many waters. When God speaks, His glory sounds like thunder crashing through the spiritual realms. It changes things! It shakes things up! Proceeding praise, which comes from God and flows through our lives, is like many waters. It is like the thunderstorm from Heaven about to release the rains of overflow in your life. When you begin to experience the sound of His voice, the overflow will come. Not only will your bills be paid, but there will also be money left to sow into the work of the Kingdom. Not only will your children be saved but their children and their children as well. You will see mountains move and strongholds pulled down, so that God may be fully glorified in your life.

11

GOVERNORS
GO TO WAR!

"But thou, O Daniel, shut up the words, and seal the book, even to the time of the end: many shall run to and fro, and knowledge shall be increased" (Dan. 12:4 KJV). The Bible says that the days are coming when people are going to be running around the globe like crazy and knowledge is going to increase. As you follow the Lord today, is there any doubt that life seems to be going faster and faster? There's no way to keep up with all the new discoveries in every area of life.

Technology has connected the world so that what happens in China is known in America within minutes. You can travel anywhere in the world within hours. You can fill your days with endless activities—or connect to the world through Facebook and the Internet on your laptop, iPad, or smartphone.

Believers are seeing prophecy being fulfilled at a higher rate of acceleration as well: *"Then said the Lord unto me, thou hast well seen: for I will hasten My word to perform it"* (Jer. 1:12 KJV). God is saying, "I will speed up, or accelerate, the performance of My Word." Let's look at Noah Webster's definition of *accelerate*:

1. To cause to move faster; to hasten; to quicken motion; to add to the velocity of a moving body. It implies previous motion or progression.

2. To add to natural or ordinary progression; as to accelerate the growth of a plant, or the progress of knowledge.

3. To bring nearer in time; to shorten the time between the present time and a future event; as to accelerate the ruin of a government; to accelerate a battle.[1]

If we apply these definitions to Jeremiah 1:12, then we see that God is going to move faster and faster in fulfilling His promises. He's going to continually increase the speed in which He moves. He's going to do this supernaturally and miraculously. God is going to shorten the length of time that it would ordinarily take to do something.

WHAT CAUSES GOD TO ACCELERATE THE PERFORMANCE OF HIS WORD?

We must go back to Jeremiah, chapter 1, to discover *how* things are accelerated.

See, I have this day set thee over the nations and over the kingdoms, to root out, and to pull down, and to destroy, and to throw down, to build, and to plant (Jeremiah 1:10 KJV).

This verse of Scripture spells out the function and mandate of the apostle and prophet today: to root out, pull down, destroy, to throw down, to build, and to plant. What happens when I'm not seeing my promise fulfilled? It's time to throw Jezebel off the train! It's time to jump on the enemy and root out some things.

If you're in a situation that's messed up, you've got to pull down the strongholds, destroy the work of the enemy, and begin building what God desires in its place. When we fulfill these six steps, we usher in Heaven on earth, and acceleration of the fulfillment of God's promises is the result. The six keys found in

Jeremiah 1:10 unlock lasting breakthrough in cities, regions, and nations.

The first four keys deal with purification and spiritual warfare. We know from Ephesians 6:10-18 that you cannot even put on the armor of God without purifying yourself. The first piece of armor is the belt of truth. Not only does this refer to believing God's Word, but it also speaks of honesty. If you are going to go to war in the spirit realm, you had better come clean and be brutally honest with God about your life.

Why is this so important? Because satan knows your weaknesses, your past sins, and everything you struggle against. He also knows everything you sweep under the rug and refuse to deal with. And when you are in the heat of battle, he will pull these things out and shoot you down with them. He will render you powerless and hopeless because of your own faults, sins, and disobedience. Can you see why the first key on the list for breakthrough is "to root out"? Apostles and prophets put a demand on the Body of Christ to root out, pull down, destroy, and throw down carnality, worldliness, and demonic influence. I believe that is why there is a great wave of repentance moving through churches today. As the apostles and prophets are set in place, the Holy Spirit flows through them to purify the Church for war—war that causes Heaven to come to earth and acceleration to be released to fulfill God's promises.

ROOT OUT

The Hebrew word for this key is *nathash,* which means "to utterly pluck up, pull out, and expel by the roots, to tear away."[2]

Just like putting on God's armor, before we can root out the works of darkness in cities, regions, and nations, we have to root out the works of darkness in our own lives and churches: *"Leave no [such] room or foothold for the devil [give no opportunity to him]"* (Eph. 4:27 AMP).

Satan cannot and will not cast out himself. If you are sleeping with the enemy, he doesn't have to submit to your authority. In fact, when it comes down to it, you really don't have authority until he has no room in your inn!

In dealing with spiritual root systems, we must remember to dig deeply. Like cutting down trees or removing weeds and other plants, if the whole root system is not removed, it will grow back. Too many times, believers only deal with the fruit of the problem. They stay on the surface and wonder why they are seeing no lasting victory over areas of sin and weakness.

It is often painful to dig deeply and face our greatest doubts, fears, sins, and trauma from the past, but it must be done to be free of the enemy's hold. We must get to the root of the problem. Then, through repentance and spiritual warfare, we can rid ourselves of satan's bitter fruit forever.

PULL DOWN

This Hebrew word is *nathats,* which means "to tear down:—beat down, break down (out), cast down, destroy, overthrow, pull down, throw down."[3]

When we are brutally honest with God and get to the root of the problem, it is time to employ the weapons of our warfare to defeat the enemy. Once he is defeated in our personal lives and in our church bodies, we can defeat him for good in territories and nations.

We use God's mighty weapons, not [mere] *worldly weapons, to knock down the* [devil's] *strongholds...* (2 Corinthians 10:4 NLT).

One of the first times my eyes were opened to the warfare that takes place over people's lives occurred when I received a vision in the fall of 1988. I was playing drums in a praise band, and when I crashed the cymbals, one of my drumsticks became a huge sword in the spirit. There were cords streaming down from the heavens and passing through the auditorium's ceiling that were attached to some people in the service. As I continued to play the drums, the sword cut through and pulled down these cords of darkness.

Then I had a vision of a young couple whom I had never seen before. The Lord revealed what they were going through and how they were bound by the enemy. I continued to play, but I also began interceding for this couple. Within minutes they walked in the back door! I had to wipe my eyes a couple of times to make sure I wasn't seeing things. I left the drums, gave an altar call, and this young couple came forward. When I ministered to them according to the vision I'd had, they were set free and saved! Glory!

Every time we engage in spiritual warfare and use this key of pulling down strongholds, we will experience new dimensions of liberty and clarity.

For though we walk in the flesh, we do not war after the flesh: (for the weapons of our warfare are not carnal, but mighty through God to the pulling down of strong holds;) casting down imaginations, and every high thing that exalteth itself against the knowledge of God, and bringing into captivity every thought to the obedience of Christ; and having in a readiness to revenge all disobedience, when your obedience is fulfilled (2 Corinthians 10:3-6 KJV).

Apostles and prophets are people of war. Battling for souls in the spirit realm is normal, everyday life to them. The Greek word for "warfare" in verse 4 is *strateia*, where we get the English word *strategy:* "military service, i.e. (figuratively) the apostolic career (as one of hardship and danger)—warfare."[4] God has given a career to apostles to cause people to come up in strategic warfare prayer so that we can possess the land and bring people to Jesus Christ.

The apostle Paul is telling us that part of his apostolic career and duty is to engage in strategic spiritual warfare and train others to do the same. Strategic warfare is part of our apostolic career. It's time for the Church to enter into battle against the forces of darkness with the host of Heaven. Every believer has a battle station to occupy.

This charge I commit unto thee, son Timothy, according to the prophecies which went before on thee, that thou by them mightest war a good warfare (1 Timothy 1:18 KJV).

According to Ephesians 6:17, your sword is the Word of God; but according to First Timothy 1:18, it is also the prophetic word of the Lord you receive to fight the good fight of faith. Remember, the Bible says that the sword is two-edged. Take up the prophecies and God's Word and wield them as a sword. Declare and decree what the Lord has said to wage a good warfare.

The two-edged sword also makes a double impact in war. While God's Word and His prophecies to you serve as a ramrod to break through into the manifestation and demonstration of what God has promised you, they are also pulling down the enemy's strongholds.

DESTROY

The Hebrew word for "destroy" even sounds bad! It is *abad,* which means "to wander away, i.e., lose oneself; to perish, break, destroy, escape, fail, lose."[5]

This is the most picturesque definition of this word I have found. *Abad* is used to describe the downfall of nations, the withering away of crops, and the fading away of strength, hope, wisdom, knowledge, and wealth. It is applied to the destruction of temples, images, and pictures. It suggests utter defeat (see Josh. 7:7), overthrowing a nation (see Deut. 28:51), and the taking of a life. *Abad* can also mean to wander about aimlessly without orientation, to be lost, whether literally or morally.

This is a very violent word! God is raising up holy destroyers to leave the enemy's works desolate. It will take nothing less than an all-out righteous assault on satan and his hordes to see lasting breakthrough in the earth. When we are finished with them, *they* should be wandering around "aimlessly without orientation," totally lost and powerless to do anything on the earth.

The Church will either destroy or be destroyed because the enemy will not stop unless we stop them: *"The thief cometh not, but for to steal, and to kill, and to destroy"* (John 10:10 KJV).

I have run into many believers who prefer to live with their heads in the sand, as if there were no such thing as spiritual warfare. Everything is all right as long as everything is all right! It has hurt my heart to see some of these people go through devastation and loss because they refused to engage in strategic spiritual warfare.

I made up my mind a long time ago that I was not going to be a boxing bag or doormat for the enemy. If he ever comes to my door, I'm ready! The Lion of the tribe of Judah will roar through me, *"You rang?!"* These days I wake up in the morning looking to destroy the works of darkness. I ask the Holy Spirit to show me someone to snatch from the fire or someone to whom I can minister healing or deliverance.

There is a movie that epitomizes the attitude of aggression we must have in the Church to defeat the enemy. It is titled, *Enough.* The story is about a battered and abused wife. She takes her child and leaves her husband to run for her life. Throughout the movie, her husband tries to find her and kill her. After one close call after another, the wife decides to stop being the victim, the one who's being chased down, and become the one on the offensive.

She discovers that her husband is planning to kill her while she is in town for a custody hearing. If she doesn't attend the hearing, the judge will rule that her daughter will have to live with the abusive father. So she wises up, begins martial arts classes, and strategizes how to take her enemy out on his own turf.

She manages to escape the creeps her husband hired to follow her and flies to the city where her husband lives. She breaks into his house while he's out and prepares to ambush him. This lady is bad to the bone! She cuts the phone lines, installs a system that blocks cell phone signals, rearranges the furniture, and rigs the lights to come on and go right back off. Then she oils herself down so that if he strikes her, the blows will slide off of her. She laces up her steel-toed boots, puts on some brass knuckles, and waits for her enemy.

When he comes home, he doesn't know what hit him! It is like the script in those old Batman shows. *Pow! Bam! Ouch!* This is a picture of the Bride of Christ doing warfare against the enemy, being so strong that the devil doesn't know what hit him. He's wandering around the earth totally disoriented, lost, and desolate—*glory!*

It's time for God's children to declare, **"Enough!"** It's time to fulfill the mission of Jesus Christ, meet the enemy on his own turf, and take him out! It's time to get oiled down with the anointing of the Holy Spirit so that nothing the enemy tries to pull on us will stick! *"The yoke shall be destroyed because of the anointing"* (Isa. 10:27 KJV).

It's time for us to put on the whole armor of God and knock the enemy down in Jesus' name!

THROW DOWN

The Hebrew word for "throw down" is *harac,* which means "to pull down or in pieces, break, destroy... overthrow, pluck down, pull down, ruin."[6]

For the arms of our warfare [are] not fleshly, but powerful according to God to [the] overthrow of strongholds (2 Corinthians 10:4 Darby).

Once you root out, pull down, and destroy the enemy, it's time to throw him down. You see it's one thing to beat the snot out of the enemy; it's another thing to dethrone enemies and send them packing! It's one thing to win a few battles; it's another thing to win the war. If you've fought this hard for this long, you might as well go ahead and have some fun with it!

Take your seat in heavenly places with Christ Jesus; gather up all the roots, cords, and strongholds of the enemy and then throw them down. Enforce the work of Jesus by completely stripping the principalities and powers, rulers of the darkness of this world, and spiritual wickedness in high places of all authority over cities, regions, and nations. Hallelujah!

The work of the Governors of Praise is only half finished, but even now you can see how the fulfillment of God's Word is accelerated when the Body of Christ declares war on and defeats the enemy. In the next chapter, you will see how Heaven is released on earth and the how acceleration increases when God's presence and government are set in place.

ENDNOTES

1. Noah Webster's 1828 American Dictionary, "accelerate," http://www.1828-dictionary.com/d/search/word,accelerate.

2. See http://concordances.org/hebrew/5428.htm; Strong's #5428, "nathash."

3. See http://concordances.org/hebrew/5422.htm; Strong's #5422, "nathats."

4. See http://concordances.org/greek/4752.htm; Strong's #4752, "strateia."

5. See http://concordances.org/hebrew/6.htm; Strong's #6, "abad."

6. See http://concordances.org/hebrew/2040.htm; Strong's #2040, "harac."

12

GOVERNMENTAL BEACHHEADS

See, I have this day set thee over the nations and over the kingdoms, to root out, and to pull down, and to destroy, and to throw down, to build, and to plant (Jeremiah 1:10 KJV).

Many historians believe that World War II was won because America's troops established a beachhead in Normandy. From that beachhead, the Allies could receive ammunition, food, equipment, and reinforcements to further the invasion into Europe.

The apostle Paul always established a beachhead. In each town or city, he would develop a core of believers and a strategic place of operation to reach the entire area God had called him to. This was literally a safe haven where the transference of power from the kingdom of darkness to the Kingdom of Light began, where the reign of the Prince of Peace was inaugurated in that region. After the enemy has been rooted out, pulled down, destroyed, and thrown down, the apostles and prophets establish a beachhead of peace to spread the Good News of the Prince of Peace and continue to wage war for souls in the surrounding territory. Unfortunately, because there have been few apostles and prophets, the Church has rarely established beachheads. As a result, the Kingdom of God has suffered loss. Tragically, we have lost believers, casualties of war who are often young in the Lord. These losses could be avoided if prophetic strategies are acted upon by the apostolic authorities in place.

Have you ever wondered why so many believers seem to take two steps forward and three steps backward? Perhaps you have even felt this way yourself. Have you found yourself asking, *Why am I going through this same battle over and over again?*

When a resurgence of the truths of spiritual warfare began in the 1980s, we pulled down a lot of strongholds, but we didn't build and plant in the places where the strongholds had existed. Therefore, the enemy came right back after we left our prophetic prayer meetings and praise rallies and found the house empty. As a result, things often got worse than they had been before we prayed!

As usual, God's Word has the answer for us.

> *When the unclean spirit is gone out of a man, he walketh through dry places, seeking rest, and findeth none. Then he saith, I will return into my house from whence I came out; and when he is come, he findeth it empty, swept, and garnished. Then goeth he, and taketh with himself seven other spirits more wicked than himself, and they enter in and dwell there: and the last state of that man is worse than the first. Even so shall it be also unto this wicked generation* (Matthew 12:43-45 KJV).

Jesus was speaking of the individual being delivered and then filled with His Word, but in verse 45, He also was speaking this to generations. There is generational repentance and generational deliverance; there is corporate repentance and corporate deliverance. The liberation of Europe from Hitler by the Allied troops during World War II is a great example of corporate deliverance in the natural realm.

The presence of God and His order and government must *replace* the principalities and powers, the rulers of the darkness of this world, and spiritual wickedness in high places over cities, regions, and nations that have been dethroned and defeated. Otherwise, the ground that was taken in war cannot be maintained in peace. To achieve this, God uses His apostles, prophets and Governors of Praise to build and to plant where the enemy once reigned.

BUILD

In the Hebrew, the word translated "build" is *banah,* meaning "to build…obtain children, make, repair, set (up)."[1]

In Chapters 2 and 3, we saw how apostles are fathers in the faith, called to raise up sons who will be faithful to war, worship, and work for the Lord. This is part of the building that the apostles undertake. The following verses refer to both natural and spiritual sons and daughters.

> *Lo, children are an heritage of the Lord and the fruit of the womb is his reward. As arrows are in the hand of a mighty man; so are children of the youth. Happy is the man that hath his quiver full of them: they shall not be ashamed, but they shall speak with the enemies in the gate* (Psalm 127:3-5 KJV).

Earlier, we explored the covenant relationship between apostolic fathers and those they father in the faith. Now we are looking at this relationship from a different perspective, a governmental perspective. These sons and daughters "speak with the enemies in the gate." The gate is the seat of government in a city or territory. And the Hebrew word for "speak" is *dabar*, meaning command, declare, warn, threaten, lead away, or put to flight.[2] These definitions speak of governmental authority.

> *That in blessing I will bless thee, and in multiplying I will multiply thy seed as the stars of the heaven, and as the sand which is upon the sea shore; and thy seed shall possess the gate of his enemies; and in thy seed shall all the nations of the earth be blessed; because thou hast obeyed My voice* (Genesis 22:17-18 KJV).

In this passage of Scripture, God is telling Abraham that he will have spiritual seed (the Church) and natural seed (the nation of Israel). Believers have natural "seed" and spiritual "seed," natural sons and daughters and spiritual sons and daughters. God willing, our natural seed will serve God and also be our spiritual seed. They will literally "possess the gate" of our enemies.

> *Listen, O isles, unto Me; and hearken, ye people, from far; the Lord hath called me from the womb; from the bowels of my mother hath He made mention of*

my name. And He hath made my mouth like a sharp sword; in the shadow of His hand hath He hid me, and made me a polished shaft; in His quiver hath He hid me; and said unto me, Thou art my servant, O Israel, in whom I will be glorified (Isaiah 49:1-3 KJV).

The apostles' sons and daughters do spiritual warfare to affect nations so that the harvest of souls can be reaped. The governmental authority of the apostles releases these gifts like arrows.

In Judges 6, Gideon tore down the altars of Baal and built an altar to the Lord. In spiritual warfare, we tear down the strongholds of the enemy and build altars to the Lord in their place.

For he took away the altars of the strange gods, and the high places, and brake down the images, and cut down the groves: and commanded Judah to seek the Lord God of their fathers, and to do the law and the commandment. Also he took away out of all the cities of Judah the high places and the images: and the kingdom was quiet before him. And he built fenced cities in Judah: for the land had rest, and he had no war in those years; because the Lord had given him rest. Therefore he said unto Judah, Let us build these cities, and make about them walls, and towers, gates, and bars, while the land is yet before us; because we have sought the Lord our God, we have sought Him, and He hath given us rest on every side. So they built and prospered (2 Chronicles 14:3-7 KJV).

The essence of apostolic building is found in prayer and worship, which we will cover in later chapters. But you can see from this passage in Second Chronicles how building altars to the Lord establishes peace and brings prosperity. The apostles and prophets are the governmental foundation that brings God's presence and order into the land through prayer and worship. This releases Heaven on earth giving supernatural acceleration for the fulfillment of the Word of the Lord

Why?

Because God now inhabits the land instead of the forces of darkness. *"But Thou art holy, O Thou that inhabitest the praises of Israel"* (Ps. 22:3 KJV).

PLANT

The Hebrew word *nata* means "to plant or to fix," to literally strike something into the ground so deeply that it is fastened there forever.[3] There is one weapon of our warfare that is two-edged: the sword of the Spirit pulls out the roots of the strongholds of the enemy and at the same time plants God's truth deep into the land.

And I have put My words in thy mouth, and I have covered thee in the shadow of Mine hand, that I

may plant the heavens, and lay the foundations of
the earth, and say unto Zion, Thou art My people
(Isaiah 51:16 KJV).

When we proclaim God's Word, we are planting
Heaven on earth! Angels are just waiting for us to
speak His Word so they can assist us. And notice that
God puts His words in our mouths. This is referring
to prophetic proclamation. We are to proclaim and
declare the Word of the Lord. We are to prophesy
His will and wisdom into the earth.

PROACTIVE FAITH BRINGS HEAVEN TO EARTH

Apostolic believers continually get in the face of
the enemy and declare, "You're not going to have my
stuff. You're not going to have my blessings. You're not
robbing my family members, my neighbors, or my co-
workers of their salvation. Get off my land. Get out
of my territory. I'm a child of the King, and this is the
King's domain."

When we get fed up with the set up and begin to
deal with the enemy, Heaven comes to earth and acceleration happens. Pacifists who wait for a blessing will
never see it. If you want acceleration of your promises, then you have to begin to accelerate yourself in
faith. You have to put your foot on the Word and move

in the Spirit. Pick up the pace of the race. Prophesy. Pray in the spirit.

Acceleration comes when we stand in faith and release what God is saying in this hour. He sees our faith and His heart leaps! He doesn't see our need—He sees our faith.

FAITH BRINGS ACCELERATION

God is not moved by our needs but by our faith. I could take you all over the world where people are in need, and you could clearly see that God is not moved by their needs. But when somebody arises who has faith in the midst of the need, God responds to that faith. And so it is with you and me.

Are you getting stressed about your situation? Maybe it's your finances, your health, or your job. Imagine you're in the ocean, swimming toward your destination. Your stress is sending blood into the water, and the sharks (the devils) are biting at you. When demons see the fear, doubt, unbelief, and stress, they attack.

You have to go to war and release that stress to God—root it out, pull it down, destroy it, and throw it down—and then build an altar of worship and plant the Word of God by declaring that you're too blessed to be stressed!

The Bible declares in Romans 10:17 that faith comes by hearing God's Word. It also tells you in Jude 20 that praying in the Spirit causes faith to rise up in your spirit. So fill yourself with the Word of God and pray in tongues to defeat stress and worry. You're filled with the Holy Spirit. You have God's Word. And if God be for you, who can be against you? (See Romans 8:31.)

If God is in you, He is greater than the devil and all the demons in the world. There has to be a stirring on the inside of you. Your spirit man may be crying out, "I know this looks bad right now, but just like Paul and Silas, I'm going to have faith. I'm going to sing and praise God in the midst of this situation, and He will turn it around."

I know your religious mind is arguing with me. You're looking at your situation and saying, "Well, I haven't come into anything but a bunch of pain and debt and trouble. I don't know what's going on."

I'm going to tell you the truth. If you continue to keep that mindset, you will wander in the desert just like the children of Israel. If all this instruction only incites you to argue with the Word of God, then you'll wander. And God will raise up another one just like you to grab hold of His Word, believe His promises, and go forward.

None of us is the "only one." God will say, "Saul, move out of the way; it's time for a David to arise. Eli, go; it's time for a Samuel to arise!" He will choose another person. God's Kingdom is not hinged on you fulfilling your divine destiny. God's Kingdom is sure. If you don't fulfill your destiny, there will be lives that will not be touched and there will be things that you should have done that could not have been done without you. But God's Kingdom will still stand strong.

The children of Israel did not believe. Instead, they complained and wandered, but that didn't negate the promise of God that Israel would possess the Promised Land. There was a generation that had to pass away. And I'm concerned in my spirit that when the Word of the Lord comes to you, you immediately agree with it—but when you don't see results the next week, you get angry and begin to complain. Eventually, you're in unbelief. You're just like the children of Israel who didn't go into the Promised Land.

While it is said, Today if ye will hear His voice, harden not your hearts, as in the provocation. For some, when they had heard, did provoke: howbeit not all that came out of Egypt by Moses. But with whom was He grieved forty years? was it not with them that had sinned, whose carcasses fell in the wilderness? And to whom sware He that they should not enter into His rest, but to them that believed not? So we see that they could not enter in because of unbelief (Hebrews 3:15-19 KJV).

Spiritual warfare and building and planting to maintain peace takes patience and faith. There's a process to obtain the promise. Sometimes you have to go through difficult times to get something and to go someplace. If there's no test, there will be no testimony. If there's no trial, there's no reason to use your faith. *Don't run from place to place ignoring the instruction and correction of the Lord.*

The Bible says that in the last days there will be a famine of the hearing of the Word of the Lord. It doesn't say there will be a famine of the Word of the Lord. It said there will be a famine of the *hearing* of the Word of the Lord. That means people who don't want to hear the Word God's giving them will run and find somebody who tells them what they want to hear. This is the opposite of apostolic order! (See Second Timothy 4:3.)

The Bible says that God hastens to perform *His* Word.

God doesn't hasten to perform His Word for those who refuse to war.

God doesn't hasten to perform His Word for people who will not build or plant.

God doesn't hasten to perform His Word for people who sit and wait for things to happen.

God doesn't hasten to perform His Word for people who complain.

God doesn't hasten to perform His Word for people who doubt and fall into unbelief.

God doesn't hasten to perform His Word for people who are moved by what they see.

God hastens to perform His Word—there is acceleration to the fulfillment of His promises—for those who walk in proactive faith. Through all the rooting out, pulling down, destroying, throwing down, building, and planting, they move forward believing that God watches over His Word to perform it.

Your Daily Role in Acceleration

If you want to see God hasten His Word to perform it in your life, there are some things you need to do. We've talked about apostolic access and the importance of coming into order and unity in the Body of Christ. We've seen the apostolic function of defeating the enemy and building the Kingdom of God. When that happens, God hastens His Word to perform it. But each believer has a vital role to perform.

How much time are you spending in prayer?

How much time are you spending in praise and worship?

How much time are you fasting?

How much time are you standing before God saying, "God, I want to see this Word come to pass"?

Do you believe the prophetic utterances that have been spoken over your life, and are you bombarding the heavens with them?

Are you dispatching angels, or are your angels just sitting, twiddling their thumbs in a corner?

What are you doing with what God has given you—gifts, talents, resources?

If you'll agree with God's Word and the words of prophecy about your life, you're going to see momentum in His promises being fulfilled.

You come up higher by prayer, praise, and meditating on God's Word. You penetrate the heavens and execute change in the spirit realm by prayer, praise, and prophecy in the presence of God. And when you do this, you step into another dimension of God's power and glory, and things begin to speed up in the natural realm.

The Word of God tells us, *"These signs shall follow them that believe"* (Mark 16:17 KJV). It didn't say these signs shall follow Kathryn Kuhlman, Benny Hinn, and Smith Wigglesworth. If you'll get passionate and aggressive in prayer, praise, and God's Word, you'll see acceleration come to your call, your destiny. Next year, when you look back, you're going to see how those things that have eluded you in the past have come into your hands.

There are believers who are about to go into warp speed. I feel it! Some are about to take quantum leaps in God. As you spend time in His presence and agree with His Word, you're going to break through the walls that have been holding you back. Then nothing can resist you because you are arising as a Governor of Praise.

ENDNOTES

1. See http://concordances.org/hebrew/1129.htm; Strong's #1129, "banah."

2. See http://concordances.org/hebrew/1696.htm; Strong's #1696, 1697; "dabar."

3. See http://concordances.org/hebrew/5193.htm; Strong's #5193, "nata."

13

GOD'S TIME TWINS: SUDDENLY AND IMMEDIATELY

And at midnight Paul and Silas prayed, and sang praises unto God: and the prisoners heard them. And suddenly there was a great earthquake, so that the foundations of the prison were shaken: and immediately all the doors were opened, and every one's bands were loosed (Acts 16:25-26 KJV).

As you arise, like Paul and Silas, as Governors of Praise, God will release His Time Twins: *Suddenly* and *Immediately*. They are going to open doors that give you opportunities and breakthrough like you've never known. *Suddenly* is going to shift things, and *Immediately* is going to open doors! You're going to walk through doors that have been shut and experience favor like never before.

Suddenly and *Immediately* are about to rain on the devil's parade. He thought he had you backed up against the wall. But *Immediately* is coming to open the door and loose you from all bonds.

Are you tired of being bound up? Are you tired of seeing your family, friends, and nation bound up?

And the keeper of the prison awaking out of his sleep, and seeing the prison doors open, he drew out his sword, and would have killed himself, supposing that the prisoners had been fled. But Paul cried with a loud voice, saying, Do thyself no harm: for we are all here. Then he called for a light, and sprang in, and came trembling, and fell down before Paul and Silas, and brought them out, and said, Sirs, what must I do to be saved? And they said, Believe on the Lord Jesus Christ, and thou shalt be saved, and thy house. And they spake unto him the word of the Lord, and to all that were in his house. And he took them the same hour of the

*night, and washed their stripes; and was baptized, he
and all his, straightway* (Acts 16:27-33).

When *Suddenly* and *Immediately* show up, souls are
saved and bonds are loosed! I don't know what you're
going through, but *Suddenly* and *Immediately* are about
to tag team and they're going to hop on the devil for
you. They're going to take care of that circumstance
or situation.

You may be thinking, *Well, Joshua, you haven't been
through anything. Everything goes all right for you. You don't
have any problems. You just write books, preach; people get all
excited, and they give you lots of money.*

This is what happens when you're a preacher. People don't think you have any problems or needs. They
don't believe you've had to live what you're preaching.
Well, I have been through some things, and I can tell
you what *not* to do!

DISOBEDIENCE HOLDS BACK
SUDDENLY AND *IMMEDIATELY*

Have you ever been restrained? You haven't truly
been restrained until you've been restrained by God.
God has taken me through some hard times. We were
living in a city where we were preaching, on the ra-
dio, making dynamic music, winning lots of souls for
Jesus, and living in a nice house. Then God moved us

to another city, sat me down, and told me not to do anything. "Don't start a church. Don't call a meeting. Don't go anywhere and preach. Don't get a job. I'll provide for you."

Now I had two houses in two cities to pay for, a wife and children to feed and clothe, and no income. You're probably thinking that the ravens fed us. The birds just dropped money from the sky to pay my rent. Every day I went out to my money tree and took it off the tree.

But that didn't happen.

You probably are thinking that somebody I prophesied over, somebody I prayed over, somebody that I blessed over all the years of traveling throughout America and the nations got a revelation from God and sent me some money.

But that didn't happen either.

Finally, after I needed God to show up and the bills were past due, we got a call to minister, and the Lord provided the money to pay both house payments and all of our bills! We all rejoiced like crazy, but there was still that frustration: *God, why didn't You do that three days ago?*

Have you ever been there?

That's when the Holy Spirit revealed to me that disobedience holds up your *Suddenly* and *Immediately*. There were things that God had told me to do, but for whatever reason, I delayed doing them. My delays in obedience caused delays in obedience in others. The Lord showed me that there were several people He had tapped on the shoulder and asked them to send me money, but they didn't do it. It wasn't too hard to see what had happened. Because I didn't do something for somebody else, those who were supposed to do something for me didn't do it.

You reap what you sow!

My wife and I decided that from that point on, if God told us to do something, we were going to do it right then. If He woke us up in the middle of the night and told us to give someone a hundred dollars, we'd go to their house that night. Why? Because we wanted to move into a *Suddenly* and *Immediately* season. Since we made this commitment, we have experienced tremendous blessing and favor in our lives.

ABOUT THIS TIME TOMORROW

Elisha said, "Hear the word of the Lord. This is what the Lord says: About this time tomorrow, a seah of flour will sell for a shekel and two seahs of barley for a shekel at the gate of Samaria" (2 Kings 7:1 NIV).

In Second Kings 6 we read one of the most horrifying stories. There was such poverty and famine in the land that some people were eating their own children. It's hard to fathom such hopelessness and despair.

In the midst of all this poverty and difficulty, the prophet Elisha prophesied that "about this time tomorrow" things would not be the same. He told the people to get ready because things were going to turn around! They were going to move from poverty to prosperity, from lack to abundance.

Like many religious people of our day, there was an unbelieving believer in the midst who spoke up and expressed his feelings of doubt and unbelief. The prophet told him, "You will see it, but you won't access it." The word of the Lord spoken through the prophet came to pass, and they experienced a breakthrough at the same time on the next day!

What happened to the unbelieving believer? He saw the fulfillment of the word, but he did not partake of it.

Now the king had put the officer on whose arm he leaned in charge of the gate, and the people trampled him in the gateway, and he died, just as the man of God had foretold when the king came down to his house. It happened as the man of God had said to the king: "About this time tomorrow, a

*seah of flour will sell for a shekel and two seahs
of barley for a shekel at the gate of Samaria." The
officer had said to the man of God, "Look, even if
the Lord should open the floodgates of the heavens,
could this happen?" The man of God had replied,
"You will see it with your own eyes, but you will not
eat any of it!" And that is exactly what happened
to him, for the people trampled him in the gateway,
and he died* (2 Kings 7:17-20 NIV).

If you desire to partake of the promises of God,
then you must believe God and those He sends into
your life.

We see God's 20/20 plan for our lives in Second
Chronicles 20:20. The Word declares, *"Believe in the
Lord your God, so shall ye be established; believe His proph-
ets, so shall ye prosper."*

When we believe God's prophets, we will prosper. There are too many non-prophet organizations in
the Church today! Because they are non-prophet, they
are non-profit. They profit little for the Kingdom of
God because they won't receive God's apostles and
prophets. Let's be like those in Second Kings 7 who
believed, and we will enter into the dimension called
"About this time tomorrow!"

14

POISED FOR
POSSESSION

*And I will give unto thee the keys of the king-
dom of heaven: and whatsoever thou shalt
bind on earth shall be bound in heaven: and
whatsoever thou shalt loose on earth shall be
loosed in heaven* (Matthew 16:19 KJV).

*The key of the house of David I will lay on
his shoulder; so he shall open, and no one
shall shut; and he shall shut, and no one
shall open* (Isaiah 22:22).

THE MASTER KEY—THE KEY OF DAVID!

Have you ever asked yourself why so many people seem unable to possess their God-given promises? Have you grown tired of religious reruns and merry-go-round ministries? Are you asking questions like the little old lady in the Wendy's commercial, "Where's the beef?"

Where is the harvest?

Where are the signs and wonders, miracles, and healings?

Why are there so many lonely seats in churches today?

If these are the questions you are asking, then you are among the company of many who, like myself, have a holy dissatisfaction for wasting time wandering aimlessly in the wilderness.

Child of God, you are called to possess! You have not come to the Kingdom for such a time as this to be a wilderness walker. You have been chosen to enter in and possess the land! You are called to be a Promise Possessor!

How can we release Heaven on earth? How can we arise and possess the land? How will the Church enter into the reaping anointing to gather the greatest harvest of all time? According to the Word of God, we open doors with the Key of David, and through rebuilding the tabernacle of David, we position our-selves for possession.

POISED FOR POSSESSION

In that day will I raise up the tabernacle of David that is fallen, and close up the breaches thereof; and I will raise up his ruins, and I will build it as in the days of old: that they may possess the remnant of Edom, and of all the heathen, which are called by My name, saith the Lord that doeth this (Amos 9:11-12 KJV).

After this I will come back, and will rebuild the house of David...so that the rest of men may seek the Lord (Acts 15:16-17 AMP).

These Scriptures vividly reveal that once we set out to co-labor with Jesus in building the tabernacle of David, we will literally enter into a reaping anoint-ing that is unprecedented. Revelation abounds to me regarding the tabernacle of David, but before I share some of these truths, I need to express the importance of what you are about to read.

In 1998, I began fervently seeking the mind of God for His blueprint for the Church. I was pastoring a young church and was desperately longing for His move to come forth. Like many others, I had been hungry to usher in God's design, pattern, and "original" model for the Church. Shortly thereafter, I began teaching a series entitled, "Apostolic Blueprints for the 21st-Century Church." In this series I gave an acronym for the word *design* to reveal what I believe is a major portion of the blueprint for the Church.

DESIGN

D = Davidic Order of Worship and Intercession (rebuilding the tabernacle of David)

E = Elisha's Expression of the Double Portion Anointing (mentoring, discipleship)

S = Sending Factor

I = International Vision

G = Governments and the Governmental Church

N =Nonconformist (defying the lie of separation of church and state)

What I will share now is a part of what God revealed to me about the first letter of the acronym: D = Davidic Order of Worship and Intercession.

In order for us to understand Davidic order, we need to find out what exactly the tabernacle of David is and how we can see it rebuilt in our cities and nations. We get a picture of how King David received the pattern for the tabernacle of David in Second Samuel, chapter 6. Like many "Uzzah-friendly" churches are finding out today, David learned the hard way that you cannot bring the presence of God on a cart!

The "cart" is humankind's thinking and ways. The cart is in many churches today and comes in the form of programs, good ideas, popularity contests, politics, and traditions of men. The death of Uzzah, whose name means "strength," clearly reveals that we cannot harness, dictate, or control the move of God with our natural strength or abilities.[1]

After Uzzah's death, King David sought the Lord for direction. In Second Samuel 6:9, David asked, *"How shall the ark* [presence] *of the Lord come to me?"* (KJV). This is a question that we should be asking today.

David sent his servants to search the Scriptures to see how to move the ark, and we should do the same today. He discovered in the Word of God that the ark (presence) of the Lord must be carried on the shoulders of the priests. The Word of God declares that once King David set things in order by having the priests carry the ark and make sacrifices to God, he was able to lead all of Israel into the city in a procession of victorious praise. David danced before the

Lord with all his might, and the people shouted and played instruments. (See First Chronicles 15:26-28.)

Once the ark was safely brought back to Jerusalem, they set it in a tent that David had pitched specifically for it. Then David stationed Levites to minister before the ark (presence) of the Lord, to *record*, to *thank*, and to *praise* the Lord God of Israel continually, 24/7, 365 days a year. (See First Chronicles 16:1,4,37.)

In these passages of Scripture, we learn that the tabernacle of David was a tent that housed the ark (presence) of the Lord. In First Chronicles we read that four thousand musicians and 288 singers were stationed to minister to the Lord 24/7, 365 days a year, in intercession, praise, and worship (see 1 Chron. 23:5; 25:7).

Perhaps you are asking yourself, is this really for today, and if so, how can we rebuild it? Yes, it is for today. Starting with King David and his son Solomon, this pattern has been handed down as an eternal, heavenly pattern: *"And the pattern of all that he had by the spirit"*(1 Chron. 28:12 KJV).

In Second Chronicles 5:12-14, we see the results of Solomon's obedience to follow the pattern.

Also the Levites which were the singers, all of them of Asaph, of Heman, of Jeduthun, with their sons and

their brethren, being arrayed in white linen, hav-
ing cymbals and psalteries and harps, stood at the
east end of the altar, and with them an hundred and
twenty priests sounding with trumpets:) It came even
to pass, as the trumpeters and singers were as one, to
make one sound to be heard in praising and thanking
the Lord; and when they lifted up their voice with the
trumpets and cymbals and instruments of musick, and
praised the Lord, saying, For He is good; for His mercy
endureth for ever: that then the house was filled with
a cloud, even the house of the Lord; so that the priests
could not stand to minister by reason of the cloud: for
the glory of the Lord had filled the house of God.

Every leader who followed the pattern that David received from the Lord possessed promises and prospered. The Word of God gives accounts of seven leaders who followed this pattern of the tabernacle of David. Two of these leaders were Nehemiah and Hezekiah.

Nehemiah rebuilt the walls by building as David did. (See Nehemiah 11 and 12.)

And he [Hezekiah] did that which was right in the
sight of the Lord, according to all that David his
father had done. He in the first year of his reign,
in the first month, opened the doors of the house of
the Lord, and repaired them. And he brought in the
priests and the Levites, and gathered them together

into the east street, and said unto them, Hear me,
ye Levites, sanctify now yourselves, and sanctify the
house of the Lord God of your fathers, and carry forth
the filthiness out of the holy place (2 Chronicles
29:2-5 KJV).

Jesus and Isaiah called the tabernacle of David *"the*
house of prayer" in Matthew 21:13 and Isaiah 56:7, re-
spectively. The apostle John revealed the beauty of
the tabernacle of David in Revelation 4 and 5. In Acts
13:2, we see the priestly principle of ministering to
God as found in the tabernacle of David. In this passage leaders ministered to God and, as a result, the
apostles Paul and Barnabas were sent forth to change
the world. We find that once the tabernacle of David
was rebuilt, God's glory overtook cities and nations.
As this happens in the Church today, we will reap
the greatest harvest of souls that this world has ever
known.

The only way for us to rebuild the tabernacle of
David is to create a habitation in which God can dwell.
We do so through intense, corporate praise and wor-
ship and through united, fervent intercessory prayer.
This requires pure, sincere hearts of men and women
who will set their eyes on the Lord.

What will we possess by rebuilding the tabernacle
of David?

In that [this] day will I raise up the tabernacle of David that is fallen, and close up the breaches thereof; and I will raise up his ruins, and I will build it as in the days of old: That they may possess the remnant of Edom, and of all the heathen, which are called by My name, saith the Lord that doeth this. Behold, the days come, saith the Lord, that the plowman shall overtake the reaper, and the treader of grapes him that soweth seed; and the mountains shall drop sweet wine, and all the hills shall melt. And I will bring again the captivity of My people of Israel, and they shall build the waste cities, and inhabit them; and they shall plant vineyards, and drink the wine thereof; they shall also make gardens, and eat the fruit of them. And I will plant them upon their land, and they shall no more be pulled up out of their land which I have given them, saith the Lord thy God (Amos 9:11-15).

Here are just five of the many blessings that can be received when we position ourselves to possess by rebuilding the tabernacle of David:

We will Possess the Harvest! (souls, souls, souls)

We will Possess New Wine! (refreshing, renewal, and revival)

We will Possess, Rebuild, and Inhabit Cities! (city transformation)

We will Possess Provision! (and the devil won't be able to steal it)

We will Possess the Land! (forever, never to be evicted)

Are you ready to possess the harvest? Are you thirsty for the new wine of the Holy Spirit? Would you like to be a part of transforming your city? Does living in the land of more than enough sound good? Are you tired of being a wilderness walker? If so, trade your sandals in for mountain boots and arise as a promise possessor today. Let's arise with a Davidic anointing as Nehemiah and Hezekiah did, wielding the sword of praise with one hand and the trowel of prayer with the other hand. Together we will rebuild the walls of the tabernacle of David and possess the land!

Rebuilding the tabernacle of David is not just a lofty idea for the corporate Body of Christ; it is for you personally, as you walk through your life and ministry.

What should you do when you've done all you can do and nothing is happening?

What should you do when life throws you a really bad deal?

What should you do when things are going so fast and furious that you have to stop and think a minute to remember your name?

BUILD GOD A HABITATION OF PRAISE!

Lift your hands up and praise Him when it doesn't look good. When it doesn't look right, feel right, and you don't see anything happening, praise Him. If you fill your mouth with praise and let the fruit of your lips bring thanksgiving and honor unto the name of Jesus—no matter what you're going through— you'll get access to places and people; you'll see an acceleration of the promises of God; and you'll see abundance flow in so you can fulfill your destiny.

Things that have been held up will be released. Things that have been delayed will be demonstrated before your eyes. Why? Because you have gone to war in the heavenlies by praising and worshiping God.

PRAISE IS WARFARE

And Judah also shall fight at Jerusalem; and the wealth of all the heathen round about shall be gathered together, gold, and silver, and apparel, in great abundance (Zechariah 14:14 KJV).

Judah means "praise." Praise will fight. I'm talking about battle-cry praise. Praise that wages war. Not wimpy praise, where you're thinking of all the things you could be doing or will be doing. I'm talking about focused, intense, passionate praise. The only way you're going to see breakthrough is if you lift up praise with your whole heart and all your strength.

When you throw your entire being into praise, your hands are weapons. The Bible says that the Lord teaches our hands to war, to fight. When you clap your hands as praise to God, you're smiting the enemy. When you pick up your feet and begin to dance in praise to the Lord, you're putting the devil under your feet. You're making the enemy your footstool.

In the boxing ring, the one who lifts his hands at the end is the winner. The fighter who's got his hands in the air, jumping up and down, is the victor. When you praise and worship God in the midst of your battle, you become *more* than a conqueror.

Jesus is the conqueror because He kicked out the door of the tomb and rose triumphantly. That makes you and me more than conquerors every time we lift our hands, especially when we're tired and scared and need a miracle! We're saying, "No matter what the odds, we're more than conquerors because of Jesus Christ!" (See Romans 8:37.)

Maybe you only lift your hands in praise when you get something. It's great to praise and thank God when you get something. But what if you need something? If you need something, lift your hands up and give Jesus praise. If you'll give Him praise, then you're going to see your enemies flee from you and your God arise: *"Let God arise, let His enemies be scattered"* (Ps. 68:1).

How does God arise?

He arises through the praises of His people. When we lift Him up, He rises in our midst and puts our enemies to flight. He sets an ambush for our enemies.

When you begin to praise God, you lift a two-edged sword. Your voice of praise to God pierces the heavens, and the heavens cannot hold back your blessings. Why? Because your hands are up, your voice is lifted, your feet are dancing, you're praising God, and the devil is fleeing. When the enemy comes in one way, the Bible says he's got to flee seven ways. (See Deuteromony 28:7.) He's all beside himself! He can't even find himself when he leaves you!

Govern Your Soul, and You'll Govern the Heavenlies

The only way to govern the heavenlies and possess territories for the Lord is to first govern your own soul. You must take charge of your mind, will, and emotions through the power of the Holy Spirit.

Soul Control

I call this Soul Control! If you don't control your soul, it will control you. Remember you are a spirit who possesses a soul that lives in a body. Keep that in order, and you'll conquer new territory every day. Self-government will increase spiritual authority to reign and rule in life. As you govern your soul, you will soar higher as a Governor of Praise. When you begin subjecting your feelings and emotions to God's Word, you'll see greater results than you've ever seen before.

If you've never done this, at first when you praise God and you don't feel like it, your mind's going to say, "You're crazy. You're a hypocrite. You don't feel any of this."

Then you need to say, "No, I don't walk by feelings. I don't walk by sight. I walk by faith, and I'm going to praise Him anyway!"

Maybe you're thinking, *Well, if the Lord will do this miracle, then I'll praise Him.*

But the Lord says, "You praise Me, and I'll do it."

What do you think a sacrifice of praise is, anyway? A sacrifice is when you don't want to. A sacrifice is when you don't feel like it. Your body hurts, your heart aches, someone just got on your last nerve— and you're going to praise God. That's a sacrifice.

Anybody can praise God when they feel good. Anybody can praise God when everything's going all right—and we should. "Well, praise God, I have money in the bank. Praise God, I'm getting married. Praise God, I got a promotion." But what about when you don't have a job? What about when you don't have a place to live? What about when you don't have a friend who'll listen? Are you going to praise Him then?

Everybody's mad at you. Nobody likes you. Your family's rejecting you, and you say, "God, I thank You that I've got a family in Heaven. I'm in Your family right here on earth. I've got Jesus in my heart, my Father's on the throne, and the Holy Spirit is helping me. He's my Comforter and Friend."

The enemy tries you because you start pressing through on God's Word. That's when you begin meeting some resistance. Your mind says, "Hey, I didn't have all this hell when I wasn't fighting. I didn't have all this trouble when I wasn't trying to do anything for God. As long as I just peacefully coexisted with the devil, just compromised with everybody, everything was going all right. I'm going to go back to the way it used to be."

Remember the way it used to be? You weren't happy. You weren't fulfilling your destiny. You were just taking up space, sucking air, and going nowhere. But now you're fighting, you're pursuing, you're moving—and you're facing some resistance. The point of resistance is not the place to stop!

PRAISE GETS YOU THROUGH THE PAIN

If you press through when you don't feel like it, if you'll give God praise when things aren't going right, things will begin to turn around. I know you're going through situations and facing circumstances where you need a breakthrough. The only way to break through is to praise your way through. It's not going to happen if you just talk about it. It's not going to happen if you just wish it. It's not going to happen if you just think about it. You're going to have to open up your mouth and praise the King of kings. Lift up your hands, shout, stomp, and dance!

ENDNOTE

1. See http://concordances.org/hebrew/5798.htm; Strong's #5798, "Uzzah."

15

GOVERNMENTAL PRAYERS AND DECREES

PRAYER BRINGS HEAVEN TO EARTH

For though we walk in the flesh, we do not war after the flesh: (For the weapons of our warfare are not carnal, but mighty through God to the pulling down of strong holds) (2 Corinthians 10:3-4 KJV).

This verse is a picture of apostolic prayer, prayer that wars against the powers of darkness so that the veil of blindness they have over people, cities, and nations is removed. Then the truth of the Gospel can be released and received.

I'm going to declare something about the time we're living in. I believe that not since the first century has the Church hit her knees as she is doing now. I believe we are in the hour where prayer is going to bring Heaven to earth and sweep nations into the Kingdom of God.

Why do I say this? Because believers are really seeking the mind and heart of the Father. We're hearing what He wants to have happen in the earth, and we're not praying little, "Please God, please, if it be Thy will, please" prayers. Instead, we're coming out of our prayer closets and showing up at prayer meetings to declare His apostolic, prophetic decrees that tear down the strongholds of the enemy and release the Word of the Lord into the earth: *"Ask of Me, and I will surely give the nations as Your inheritance"* (Ps. 2:8 NASB). Apostolic prayer asks for nations, because that's what God wants.

You serve a big God who loves to grant big requests. He desires for you to ask for the big things. He is raising up prayer warriors like Hannah in this hour. They will not let go of the horns of the altar until they see God's will done on earth as it is in Heaven. To

Hannah, her destiny was to be fruitful and multiply according to God's Word, and she refused to budge until she saw His Word manifested in her life.

> *So Hannah rose up after they had eaten in Shiloh, and after they had drunk. Now Eli the priest sat upon a seat by a post of the temple of the Lord. And she was in bitterness of soul, and prayed unto the Lord, and wept sore. And she vowed a vow, and said, O Lord of hosts, if Thou wilt indeed look on the affliction of Thine handmaid, and remember me, and not forget Thine handmaid, but wilt give unto Thine handmaid a man child, then I will give him unto the Lord all the days of his life, and there shall no razor come upon his head. And it came to pass, as she continued praying before the Lord, that Eli marked her mouth* (1 Samuel 1:9-12).

This is what is happening in the Church right now. There is a company of intercessors, a people of warfare, who are praying unlike people who prayed before. They're entering into new realms of spiritual warfare, and many of the religious and traditional folk do not understand what they are doing. Like Eli, they are marking the mouths of those who are prayer warriors. But we must keep praying, for out of our spirits our prayers will give birth to a Samuel generation the likes of which this world has never known!

And Eli said unto her, How long wilt thou be drunken? put away thy wine from thee. And Hannah answered and said, No, my lord, I am a woman of a sorrowful spirit: I have drunk neither wine nor strong drink, but have poured out my soul before the Lord. Count not thine handmaid for a daughter of Belial: for out of the abundance of my complaint and grief have I spoken hitherto. Then Eli answered and said, Go in peace: and the God of Israel grant thee thy petition that thou hast asked of Him (1 Samuel 1:14-17 KJV).

Hannah continued in prayer even though the religious order marked her and accused her of being drunk. We must have this same excellent spirit if we are going to come up higher. God honored her faith, her perseverance, and her courage. Access was granted, and the great prophet Samuel was born to her.

In the process of praying to obtain the promise, Hannah came up higher!

And she said, Let thine handmaid find grace in thy sight. So the woman went her way, and did eat, and her countenance was no more sad (1 Samuel 1:18 KJV).

When God grants you access and you come up higher, you've got to remove the sackcloth and ashes and praise Him. Worship the Lord over His promise!

And they rose up in the morning early and worshipped before the Lord, and returned, and came to their house to Ramah: and Elkanah knew Hannah his wife; and the Lord remembered her. Wherefore it came to pass, when the time was come about after Hannah had conceived, that she bare a son, and called his name Samuel, saying, Because I have asked him of the Lord (1 Samuel 1:19-20 KJV).

All of this happened because Hannah prayed. She asked the Lord for a son, and her prayers gave birth to the prophet Samuel, who had an anointing to shift the heavens.

Your prayers will shift the heavens too.

God is raising up Hannahs who will give birth to Samuels! I see entire congregations being transformed by the power of the Spirit into Hannah Houses. These Hannah Houses will give birth to the greatest prophetic generation this world has ever known. I hear the Lord say, "Hannah, Hannah, come forth and give birth to my Samuels in the earth." Can you hear Him calling? Hannah, Hannah, come forth? I hear the Lord saying, "Samuel, Samuel, yes, a Samuel generation is arising."

Samuels are shifters! They are a shift generation, and wherever they go, they shift atmospheres. Whatever they prophesy comes to pass.

Samuel prophesied, and not one word fell to the ground. Samuel shifted the priesthood, and he shifted governments. He prophesied the end of Eli and his son's priestly service. Samuel prophesied the end of Saul's reign and the beginning of David's rule. So it is with this Samuel generation arising today. These Samuel shifters are shifting administrations within both the church and civil government.

I hear the Spirit of the Lord saying, *Shift!* God is shifting gears, and we must shift with Him. This shift will take us to the next level. There is a shift that we must embrace in order to reap the last harvest.

This is not just a generational shift, but something that we must discern in our everyday lives in order for us to cross over and possess our promised land. Many leaders have been stuck, and like a gear that is positioned improperly, they will burn out if they refuse to make the shifts God requires of them.

Those who will shift with God's shift will be exalted and will eat the good of the land. It is time for us to shift in the following ways.

Shift in Leadership—from Elis to Samuels, Sauls to Davids (see 2 Sam. 1:5,9-10,13,15,17). Samuels, Davids, and Joshuas are coming forth to lead the shift generation.

Paradigm Shift—from sheep to soldiers, from lambs to lions.

Shift of Focus—from the local church to the Kingdom of God.

Shift Into the Third-Day Dimension—See Ezra 5:12; 6:14-15; John 2:1-11,19-21; Hosea 6:1-3; Joshua 3.

Shift in Wealth—wealth will begin to shift into the hands of the righteous.

Shift in Structure—from man's order to God's order (see 1 Sam. 6; Eph. 2:20-22).

Shift From Shame to Fame—(see Zeph. 3:19-20).

Geographical Shift—even more movement and relocating of ministries as God rearranges seats of leadership for those who are faithful and teachable.

Shift in the Heavenlies—God is releasing new anointings and angelic forces into the earth.

Shift in Church Membership—an exodus has begun as saints flee from dead, religious churches to go where the life of the Spirit flows freely and the Word of God is truly lived. The churches that shift with God's apostolic restoration will see exponential growth. Others will decrease because they resist the moves of God or refuse to restrain spiritual children who are living in sin.

CHANGING OF THE GUARD

While ministering in Taiwan in 1997, I had the privilege of witnessing something that captivated me. It clearly illustrated a shift. It was the changing of the guard at the Chiang Kai-shek Memorial. Chiang Kai-shek was the founding president of Taiwan, and he was a Christian. As I watched the changing of the guard, the Lord revealed some things that I had never seen while watching the changing of the guard in other countries.

A statue of President Chang Kai-shek stood in the center of the main room of the memorial. Approximately 75 feet on each side of the statue, there was a soldier standing guard on top of a pedestal that looked to be about two feet in height. I watched in amazement as these two soldiers stood with their guns outstretched, facing the memorial and each other without moving a muscle.

The clock struck, and in the distance I could hear soldiers marching in unison. Those around me were saying, "They're coming; they're coming," and watched the hallway in anticipation of their arrival. I did not know until later that the distinct sound that had captivated my attention was coming from metal taps on the bottom of the soldiers' boots.

After hearing but not seeing anything for quite a while, the moment arrived, and three soldiers rounded the corner. The leading soldier had a scroll of orders beneath his arm, and the two soldiers who marched behind him had bayonets resting upon their shoulders. When they all came to a stop, the two soldiers who were standing guard simultaneously hit their guns on their pedestals and dismounted. They left their posts marching in unison: *tap, step, tap, step, tap, step.* They were at least 150 feet apart at the beginning, yet they stayed in sync and moved as one!

Marching to the center, these two soldiers joined ranks with the other three and faced the memorial with their backs to us. Suddenly they turned, facing each other. At the command of the soldier in the middle (the one with the scroll), they hit their guns on the ground and tilted them toward each other, so as to salute one another. Then, almost faster than I could blink, they changed places. They hit their guns on the floor again and tilted them forward again.

The soldiers who had the next watch (or shift) marched to the pedestals and took their posts. They hit their guns on their pedestals and tilted them toward each other. I watched as the former guards marched out of the room. On the right shoulder of each of their uniforms was a patch with a roaring lion on it.

This experience had a profound impact on me. Following are some insights I had as I witnessed the changing of the guard.

- When we are on guard, we are to be sober and vigilant.

- When it's time to *shift,* whether coming on or going off, we move the moment the clock strikes.

- Unity creates a distinct sound, and we must march together in rank and order. (See Joel 2 and 3; Psalm 133; and Ephesians 4.)

- The five soldiers represent the five-fold ministry gifts (see Eph. 4:11).

The soldier who had the scroll beneath his arm represents the apostle. Apostles are graced to establish governments, which cause divine order within the Body of Christ. When operating correctly, an apostle discerns which five-fold ministry anointing is needed for a particular situation or portion of a service, and he or she releases that person to function in his or her callings and gifts.

The other four soldiers represent the prophet, evangelist, pastor, and teacher. These four remain sensitive, so they can take their *shift* when called upon. While not on a pedestal, they are to support those who are with prayer and prepare for their next *shift* (clean and load their guns; or, in other words, study, fast, and pray).

- Shifts come more often than we think. If we're not ready, one of two things may happen:

  Those on post will stay on post too long and burn out or fall asleep on duty, which causes an opening for the enemy to come in.

  Those who are ready and willing to take their *shift* are unable to fulfill their destinies. This can cause soldiers to become disheartened and disillusioned.

- The patch with the roaring lion represents that we are being transformed from sheep into soldiers and from lambs into lions. We are authorized to enforce the dominion of the Lion of Judah.

- When the soldiers tilted their swords toward each other, they were preferring one another, releasing and empowering one another to take their *shift*.

When you begin to pray from the innermost part of your being to birth God's will into the earth in a shift, it will be a prayer of groaning and a place of travail. You are giving birth to what God wants—the nations.

Apostolic prayer brings God's order and God's orders. Apostolic prayer brings the strategies of God to defeat the enemy. Apostolic prayer brings the world to the Lord Jesus Christ!

And Samuel grew, and the Lord was with him, and did let none of his words fall to the ground (1 Samuel 3:19 KJV).

Why did none of Samuel's words fall to the ground? Samuel had learned how to pray and minister to the Lord from his mother. He only spoke what God told him to speak. He decreed the Word of the King, and it was so.

I believe nations are shifting because God's Governors of Praise are rising up in praise, prayer, and prophecy. We are placing our hands upon government officials, just as Elisha did to the King Joash of Israel, and we are receiving divine strategies to affect lasting change in the world:

And Elisha said unto him, Take bow and arrows. And he took unto him bow and arrows. And he said to the king of Israel, Put thine hand upon the bow. And he put his hand upon it: and Elisha put his hands upon the king's hands (2 Kings 13:15-16 KJV).

Being a Governor of Praise is not a profession or event; it's a lifestyle. It is a journey that will never end—until you stand before God's glorious throne at the end of your earthly life and begin your unending praise of Him face to face.

Psalm 24:6 states, *"This is Jacob, the generation of those who seek Him, who seek Your face."* Are you part of this generation of Jacob? Do you want proceeding praise to overflow from your life, blessing all those around you, as well as the world in which you live? This is a critical hour on planet Earth. We are the generation preparing for the return of the Lord Jesus Christ. This is the *kairos* season—and we are a generation that is determined to seek God's face, to know Him intimately, and to govern as He would have us upon this earth. We have had the Boomer generation; we've had the Gen Xers; and now it's time for the Governors!

GOVERNORS OF PRAISE DECREE: PROCLAIM ALOUD!

I decree and declare that God is raising up an army of Governors of Praise throughout the earth. As a Governor, I take my seat with Christ in heavenly places. I am no longer looking up at the enemy, but I assume my delegated position and I'm looking down upon the enemies of the Kingdom of God. I sit with Christ and laugh the enemy into derision. As a Governor, I wield praise as a weapon and execute the judgments of the Lord. I release the sounds of Heaven, and in the name of Jesus, I tell the devil to shut up. No weapon that's formed against me shall prosper, and every tongue that rises against me I pass sentence on now. (See Isaiah 54:17.)

Because the fire of God is burning in my life, I am too hot to handle and too bold to hold for the enemy. Jailhouses rock and prison doors open through my praise, and many captives are set free by the presence of the Lord. I penetrate through praise, prayer, and prophecy, and I'm saturated in His presence. As the rain of Heaven, I permeate with God's glory wherever I go. I have a destiny to reign and rule with Christ, to govern the heavenlies and subdue territories for the Kingdom of God. As a member of the Body of Christ and His holy congress, I pass divine legislation that thwarts the plans of darkness and releases the blessings and promises of the Lord.

I render powerless the enemy's tactics of sickness, disease, division, doubt, lack, poverty, debt, divorce, depression, deception, accusations, curses, and anything that tries to rise up against my life, my family, and the Church. I invoke the name that is above every name, the mighty and matchless name of *Jesus,* and enforce the divine decree and promises of God's Word that have been ratified by His shed blood! I appropriate the provisions, prosperity, and power of Christ's will in my life and territory. In Jesus' name, *amen.*

IN THE RIGHT HANDS, THIS BOOK WILL CHANGE LIVES!

Most of the people who need this message will not be looking for this book. To change their lives, you need to put a copy of this book in their hands.

> *But others (seeds) fell into good ground, and brought forth fruit, some a hundred-fold, some sixty-fold, some thirty-fold* (Matthew 13:8).

Our ministry is constantly seeking methods to find the good ground, the people who need this anointed message to change their lives. Will you help us reach these people?

> *Remember this—a farmer who plants only a few seeds will get a small crop. But the one who plants generously will get a generous crop* (2 Corinthians 9:6).

EXTEND THIS MINISTRY BY SOWING
3 BOOKS, 5 BOOKS, 10 BOOKS, **OR MORE TODAY,**
AND BECOME A LIFE CHANGER!

Thank you,

Don Nori Sr., Founder
Destiny Image
Since 1982

DESTINY IMAGE PUBLISHERS, INC.

"Promoting Inspired Lives."

VISIT OUR NEW SITE HOME AT
WWW.DESTINYIMAGE.COM

FREE SUBSCRIPTION TO DI NEWSLETTER

Receive free unpublished articles by top DI authors, exclusive

discounts, and free downloads from our best and newest books.

Visit www.destinyimage.com to subscribe.

Write to: Destiny Image
                   P.O. Box 310
                   Shippensburg, PA 17257-0310

Call: 1-800-722-6774

Email: orders@destinyimage.com

For a complete list of our titles or to place an order
online, visit www.destinyimage.com.

FIND US ON FACEBOOK OR FOLLOW US ON TWITTER.

www.facebook.com/destinyimage   facebook
www.twitter.com/destinyimage   twitter